Poetry as Survival

The Life of Poetry

POETS ON THEIR ART AND CRAFT

Poetry as Survival

GREGORY ORR

The University of Georgia Press

ATHENS & LONDON

Published by the University of Georgia Press
Athens, Georgia 30602
www.ugapress.org
© 2002 by Gregory Orr
All rights reserved
Designed by Kathi Dailey Morgan
Set in 10.5 on 13 Bembo by Bookcomp, Inc.

Printed digitally in the United States of America

Library of Congress Cataloging-in-Publication Data

Orr, Gregory.
    Poetry as survival / Gregory Orr.
    vii, 235 p. ; 22 cm. — (The life of poetry)
Includes index.
    ISBN 0-8203-2427-2 (alk. paper)
    ISBN 0-8203-2428-0 (pbk.   )
    1. English poetry—History and criticism.
2. American poetry—History and criticism.
3. Poetry.   I. Title.   II. Series.
PR502 .O77 2002
821.009—dc21   2002003603

Paperback ISBN-13: 978-0-8203-2428-9

British Library Cataloging-in-Publication Data available

Contents

Acknowledgments

A number of people have given me invaluable help in shaping and clarifying this book. Among those whose early encouragement and advice were essential are Adrienne Rich, Sandra Gilbert, Mark Edmundsen, and Susan Gubar. Patricia Hampl and Mary Oliver read entire, earlier versions of this text and responded with astute comments and suggestions. Others whose responses were helpful include Alan Williamson, Carol Houck Smith, Richard Wertime, Steve Berg, Sam Hamill, and David and Joan Grubin. I also wish to thank Jen Chang for her assistance in checking quotes and Barbara Ras for her superb editing.

Poetry as Survival

Everywhere and Always

It is difficult
to get the news from poems
yet men die miserably every day
for lack
of what is found there.

WILLIAM CARLOS WILLIAMS,
"Asphodel, That Greeny Flower"

As a poet, I've always hated the fact that poetry often intimidates people. Many people I know feel that poetry is a test they can only pass if they are smart enough or sensitive enough, and most fear they will fail. Many refuse the test altogether—never read poetry—for fear of failure. Somehow something has gone wrong with poetry in our culture. We have lost touch with its value and purpose, and in doing so, we have lost contact with essential aspects of our own emotional and spiritual lives.

There is something special about poetry and about lyric poetry in particular, but it's not what most people think. It's not that poetry is written by very intelligent or very sensitive people and is appreciated only by others of equal intelligence and sensitivity. What's special is quite the opposite of this elitist notion of poetry. What's special is that lyric poetry is written down or composed in every culture on the planet at this moment, which means something like one thousand different cultures and three thousand different languages. All cultures on the globe have a conception of the personal lyric. What's more, members of all these cultures feel free to write it down or compose it aloud as song or chant, whether they are from tribes in

I

the equatorial rain forests or Inuit and Eskimo in the frozen Arctic; whether they live in Paris or Buenos Aires or Beijing.

In addition to being omnipresent on the planet at this moment, lyric poetry appears to have been written and composed in every ancient or historical culture we have been able to investigate. For all we can tell, poetry may be almost as ancient as the use of language itself. Certainly, when civilizations first made use of written language, poetry was among the first things chosen to be preserved by this new technology of permanence. The Homeric epics, *The Iliad* and *The Odyssey*, transmitted orally for several centuries, were written down 2,700 years ago, shortly after the development of the Greek alphabet, and the lyric poems of Archilochus and Sappho followed soon after. In China, the collection known in the West as *The Book of Songs* or *The Book of Odes* was also transmitted orally for several centuries before being written down almost 2,500 years ago. Many of these ancient Chinese poems are lyrics that speak about things that still matter in our lives, like the love longing in this one spoken by a woman:

> Blue blue your collar,
> sad sad my heart:
> though I do not go to you,
> why don't you send word?
>
> Blue blue your belt-stone,
> sad sad my thoughts:
> though I do not go to you,
> why don't you come?
>
> Restless, heedless,
> I walk the gate tower.
> One day not seeing you
> is three months long.
> (from *The Columbia Book of Chinese Poetry*)

Archaeologists in Egypt have discovered four collections of love poetry compiled during the New Kingdom period 3,300 years ago.

Three of these "anthologies" are on papyrus fragments, the fourth was carved on the side of a stone vase. Here is a translation of one of these Egyptian poems, spoken by a male lover plotting to get his sweetheart's attention:

> I shall lie down at home
> and pretend to be dying.
> Then the neighbors will all come in
> to gape at me, and, perhaps, she will come with them.
> When she comes, I won't need a doctor,
> she knows why I am ill.

How simple such a poem is and yet how emotionally complete and amusing—how easy it is for us to enter into the situation and the speaker's feelings. And yet it was written over three thousand years ago.

It seems important to say at the outset that the kind of poem I am discussing, what I call the "personal lyric," does not by any means constitute the bulk of the world's lyric poetry legacy. For complicated reasons, personal lyrics are often not preserved with as much care as other kinds of lyrics, especially those that express and reinforce the governing religious, political, and social structures of a given society. Thus, although we encounter a powerful poet of the personal lyric at the very beginning of Greek literature, namely Sappho, most of the Western lyric tradition up until the Romantics consists of what I call "social lyrics" and "sacred lyrics" (in appendixes A and B these distinctions are explored). In the pages that follow, I'll focus on the personal lyric and a variant on the personal lyric, the transformative lyric, hoping to describe how they function in the life of the individual poet and reader. It's my belief that this kind of poem has a crucial role to play in our psychological, imaginative, and spiritual lives.

WE OFTEN EXPERIENCE the world as confusing and chaotic, especially during crises. This confusion can be outside us, in the objective conditions of our social and political lives, or it can be inside us, in the swiftly shifting world of emotions, thoughts, and memories. Even as we recognize the power of disorder in our experience, we are likely to become aware of a strong need we have to feel there is some order in the world that helps us feel safe and secure. Our day to day consciousness can be characterized as an endlessly shifting, back-and-forth awareness of the power and presence of disorder in our lives and our desire or need for a sense of order. Most of us live most of our lives more or less comfortably with the daily interplay of these two awarenesses, but in certain existential crises, disorder threatens to overwhelm us entirely. In those cases, the very integrity of the self is threatened, and its desire or ability to persist is challenged. Among the most obvious and dramatic of these upheavals we could include intense romantic passion or the sudden death of someone near and dear to us. And yet our instability is present to us almost daily in our unpredictable moods and the way memories haunt us and fantasies play themselves out at will on our inner mental screens. We are creatures whose volatile inner lives are both mysterious to us and beyond our control. How to respond to the strangeness and unpredictability of our own emotional being? One important answer to this question is the personal lyric, the "I" poem dramatizing inner and outer experience.

Human culture "invented" or evolved the personal lyric as a means of helping individuals survive the existential crises represented by extremities of subjectivity and also by such outer circumstances as poverty, suffering, pain, illness, violence, or loss of a loved one. This survival begins when we "translate" our crisis into language—where we give it symbolic expression as an unfolding drama of self and the forces that assail it. This same poem also arrays the ordering powers our shaping imagination has brought to bear on these disorderings. Thus the poem we compose (or respond to as readers) still accurately mirrors the life crisis it dramatizes, still displays life's interplay of disorder and order. But in the act of making a poem at least two crucial things have taken place that are different from ordinary life. First, we have shifted the crisis to a bearable distance from us: removed it to the symbolic but vivid world of language. Second, we have actively *made* and shaped this model of our situation rather than passively endured it as lived experience.

AND YET, THE project of poem-making I wish to describe, this active taking-hold of one's emotional life, begins with a passive receptivity, which is vividly expressed by the final lines of a poem by D. H. Lawrence:

> What is the knocking?
> What is the knocking at the door in the night?
> It is somebody wants to do us harm.
>
> No, no, it is the three strange angels.
> Admit them, admit them.
> ("Song of a Man Who Has Come Through")

The first three lines I've quoted dramatize the terror we might feel when faced with the unknown and unexpected. The final two lines respond with not only a cryptic reassurance about the identity of our visitors but also firm advice about how we must respond to them. We must overcome our fears and open our doors to them; we must admit their radiant, disturbing power into our psychic lives.

THE SURVIVAL VALUE of personal lyric is for listeners/readers as well as writers. Broadly speaking, its function is to help us express and regulate our emotional lives, which are confusing and sometimes opaque to us. This survival function of the personal lyric can be quite readily recognized when we consider that in our culture much of popular music consists of what I would consider personal lyric poetry. I am not saying that the lyrics of popular songs are as coherent or sophisticated in their patterning as poems written for the page—that's a different story, since much of a song's meaning is carried by rhythm and melody. I *am* saying that the particular songs that you love deeply help you to live just as surely as do the poems you cherish. Popular music (be it rock and roll, rhythm and blues, country, folk, or rap) has the power to express and regulate our emotions. Popular music of one kind or another is important to the subjective lives of most of us, but it is especially crucial during adolescence, when it can almost seem as if we exist from one passionately loved song to the next—as if adolescence were a series of leaps through swirling darkness in which we landed on the bright, shining stone of one song after another. I know I couldn't have made it through that part of my life without rock and roll—that is, without songs I loved intensely, songs that I felt expressed and channeled the powerful and inchoate feelings that churned inside me. I say "rock and roll" and I mean the whole field of popular song. My parents' generation survived on lyrics by Gershwin, Irving Berlin, and Cole Porter. I couldn't have lived without certain songs by Dylan and the Beatles. My youngest daughter loves Kurt Cobain and the British band Pulp. The music changes (radically) from generation to generation, but the survival function remains the same.

THAT THE DISCOVERY of poetry can have enormous transformative power is something I know from my own experience. I grew up in the 1950s in the countryside of upstate New York and had had a rifle of my own since the age of ten. When I was twelve years old I was responsible for a hunting accident in which my younger brother died. To say that I was horrified and traumatized by the event is only to state the obvious. I've written elsewhere (in poems and a memoir) about my emotional responses to this experience; I won't rehearse them here. Two years after my brother's death, my mother died suddenly, at the young age of thirty-six, after a "routine" hospital procedure. In 1965, at the age of eighteen, I worked briefly as a volunteer in the South for the Civil Rights movement and was on the receiving end of both state-organized political violence (numerous police beatings with clubs) and vigilante rage (being abducted at gunpoint in rural Alabama and held in solitary confinement for eight days). These various experiences gave me a terrifying sense of how fragile human life is, how easily and quickly people can vanish.

Since, in the hunting accident, I was the child holding the gun that killed my brother, I also acquired an enormous burden of guilt and anguish: a burden that threatened to overwhelm my adolescent ego with despair and worse. My parents were so devastated and upset by my brother's death that they were unable to offer me any consolation for my deed, or even to speak with me about it. At the time of my brother's death, a friend of the family counseled me that my brother's death was all part of God's plan, which was necessarily inscrutable to us on earth. This notion of a divine order that had the power to subsume such violent disorder didn't seem believable to me and failed to help me live through the traumatic crisis that had become my life.

Other people, including my parents, told me my brother's death was "an accident." They were right, of course, at one level. But what they did not seem to realize was that for me the word "accident" was the name of the horror that had happened, *not* a response to it—not an ordering, not a meaning. Who could live in a world composed of accidents so terrible as to leave your little brother, who was standing beside you one moment, the next moment a lifeless corpse at your feet? Unbearable word, this "accident." Unbearable world.

My twelve-year-old consciousness desperately needed meaning in order to survive what I had done. That day of my brother's death I did find, for myself and by myself, something in the Bible that spoke to my situation: the story of Cain and Abel, the one brother slaying the other in a field. This was not, on the face of it, a very consoling story to identify with, but it helped me survive the earliest part of the trauma, even if it meant that I came to secretly believe that I was Cain. At least Cain lived, I told myself; that Cain continued living after Abel's death was part of the story, part of the story's strange meaning.

At the time of my brother's death, no one proposed philosophical attitudes to me, but had they done so I doubt I would have gained any consolation or understanding from them. In my experience, the conceptualizations philosophy offers are not adequate to the sudden death of a loved one, nor the anguish in families that follows.

I lived for about four years after my brother's death without any hope at all. Nothing that I found in my culture sustained me. Even my relationship with the natural world, which had been so important to me earlier, was not enough to alter my grief, despair, and guilt. Then, thanks to Mrs. Irving, the librarian in my small public school, I discovered poetry. I had previously had a vague desire to write, but nothing had brought me to lyric poetry or the writing of it. In the small "honors English" class that Mrs. Irving taught during my senior year, she had us write all kinds of things: stories, sketches, plays, haiku. I wrote a poem one day, and it changed my life. I had a sudden sense that the language in poetry was "magical," unlike language in fiction: that it could create or transform reality rather than simply describe it. That first poem I wrote was a simple, escapist fantasy, but it liberated the enormous energy of my despair and oppression as nothing before had ever done. I felt simultaneously revealed to myself and freed of my self by the images and actions of the poem. I knew from that moment on that all I wanted to do was write poems. I knew that if I was to survive in this life, it would only be through the help of poetry. Mind you, I am not saying my early poems were good, or that I knew anything about the skill of crafting a poem—years of agonized apprenticeship were before me—but the experience of hope and pleasure was revelatory to me then and still underlies my understanding of an essential purpose and meaning of lyric poetry.

It's been my great good luck that what saved my life has, since that moment, become its main preoccupation and the source of my livelihood. I've taught the reading and writing of poetry for the past twenty-five years. Everything I've learned in that time reinforces my own experience that the personal lyric helps individual selves, both writers and readers, survive the vicissitudes of experience and the complexities and anguish of subjectivity and trauma.

Much of my book is speculative and meant to be suggestive rather than definitive. Again and again, I have a sense that I am only pointing in certain directions and that other people will see more clearly and express more lucidly what is there waiting to be identified and described. On the other hand, I've done the best I could to interrogate my intuitions and test them against the rich evidence of poems I know and love.

PART ONE

The Self, Jeopardy, and Song

CHAPTER ONE

Poised on a Mountain Peak, Floating on the Ocean

I stepped from Plank to Plank
A slow and cautious way
The Stars about my Head I felt
About my Feet the Sea.

I knew not but the next
Would be my final inch —
This gave me that precarious Gait
Some call Experience.

EMILY DICKINSON, J. 875

If we knew what the next moment held, or the next week, wouldn't we feel differently about the future? If we knew what would happen tomorrow? But we don't.

And where are the events of last week? Can we find them anywhere? Or that glorious summer day two years ago when we swam in the river? Where has it gone? Has it ceased to exist? "Où sont les neiges d'antan?"—"Where are the snows of yesteryear?"—the sixteenth-century French poet and outlaw François Villon asked in his lament that lists the names of celebrated beauties who, even as he wrote, were fading along with their fame.

I look forward into the unknown. I look backward and the moment I just inhabited has vanished as quickly as if I drove on a highway—I can barely glimpse it in the rear-view mirror, and then it has disappeared entirely.

Maybe I should look inside myself for something stable. What do I see and hear if I pause for sixty seconds to try to register what is passing through my consciousness? I see brief images—fragments of thoughts announce themselves, then sensations my body sends about its position and comfort, or about sounds and smells, and then a phrase from a song passes through and I think of someone, see his or her face and then the memory image of a house where we both were, and a sad feeling, and then one of longing, and now something else, and a voice is talking inside me also, chattering along as if it were a radio commentator. And all of this taking place in sixty seconds, and happening faster and more confusingly than I could ever communicate in something as simple and straightforward as written language.

What I'm trying to sketch here is a sense of what it feels like to be a self in the world. It's an odd thing to be a self, and stressing that oddness, for a moment, can lead us toward notions of the nature and purpose of lyric poetry. If my sketch of a self in its existential context sounds a bit melodramatic, bear with it briefly until, as Keats says, you can prove it (or disprove it) on your own pulse.

Imagine the self as a small circle in the middle of a blank page. This circle of self is bisected by a dotted vertical line that stands for the present moment, the moment we are inhabiting right now. This present moment is all that we ever really have—it is where we exist and the only place we exist. This circle of self will move forward (toward the right margin) into a succession of present moments. Behind the circle of self (toward the left margin), are all the past moments it has lived—they are gone, they have become what I'd call the Vanished Past. All the joys and terrors, the boring days and the Kodak moments—all up in smoke and the smoke itself drifted away into the blue of oblivion that is the Vanished Past. Even as you read this line, the moment in which you read the last one is irrevocably gone and with it all that you thought and felt.

And what about the future, that space to the right of the circle of self? What about the next moment that is approaching you now? You can't know what that moment holds anymore than you can know what words I will write in my next sentence. What words I will write in my next sentence. (Could you have predicted my odd and spontaneous decision to repeat those words? No more than you could predict next week's weather or the day on which you will meet a new love or your own death). The truth is, to a very great extent, we all of us live our lives with our faces pressed up against the unknown and unknowable next moment. True, the sun will (probably) rise tomorrow and many of us rightly take comfort in that certainty. And it's good that basic things are predictable— that the earth will stay below our feet and the sky above our heads (though in earthquakes that might change). But how little we really know about the future, which I here choose to call the Unknowable Next.

Behind us, the Vanished Past; before us, the Unknowable Next. And within us? Does anybody's consciousness resemble a well-ordered room—all the furniture neatly arranged, and in the dresser the socks and shirts and blouses precisely folded and the contents of our closets color-coded also? If you were to pause right now, close your eyes, and listen to your mind for sixty successive seconds, you would undoubtedly encounter a ceaseless jumble of emotions and ideas and thoughts and body sensations and memory images and a voice jabbering away like a twenty-four-hour-a-day radio station. I call this interior chaos the Buried Self because so little of it gets out. When we say "I spoke my mind about that," we don't mean that we expressed in words the actual and complete contents of our consciousness, but only a narrow thread of focused thought or emotion. The contents of our minds are like an iceberg that is 90 percent below the waterline of silence—even *we* don't know and can't keep track of what's going on inside us.

The self, in my image, is like a tiny island in a vast sea of chaos, and it's also like those conch shells you lift to your ear to hear the ocean's roar: the chaos of the sea is inside the self also.

Two Awarenesses and How They Interact

I'm not saying the bisected circle of the self is the only accurate model of the human condition. I am simply proposing it as one image of our situation, an image that deliberately emphasizes the sense of jeopardy built into the experience of being a self in the world. Why? Because I think that an awareness of the disorderly and chaotic world we inhabit is a fundamental aspect of being human. Disorder, in one form or another, presents itself to us powerfully and constantly. Besides the vanishings, inner chaos, and outer unpredictabilities I've already sketched, disorder surges up in all the primary passions—love, hate, jealousy, despair, terror, joy. And we experience disorder's power when beauty or wonder overwhelm us or ecstasy seems to dissolve the very boundaries of self. And it surrounds us in the form of lucky and unlucky accidents that can and do happen constantly in our lives. Sometimes we even go in deliberate search of vitalizing disorder, which we call adventure. But for the most part, such a heightened awareness of the role of disorder in our lives is an alarming and dismaying experience. So alarming that we could say it is unbearable.

And this unbearableness of disorder brings us to a second awareness: that each of us needs a sense of order, a sense that some patterns or enduring principles are at work in our lives. Though the tolerance for disorder varies from individual to individual, no one can live in a world of complete randomness. Each of us needs to believe that patterns and structures exist and can be made to exist. To be human is to have a deep craving for order. One of the pleasures we each take in our small daily rituals (I like to eat two pieces of whole-wheat toast for breakfast each day) is the sense of security these habits give us.

How does our deep need for orderings and pattern interact with our equally profound awareness of the power of randomness, accident, and disorder in our lives?

The awareness of disorder generates in the human mind a spontaneous ordering response. This ordering response is innate, a natural power—all human minds possess it. Why not call it "imagination" and recognize it as a fundamentally human cognitive capacity? As the poet Robert Duncan put it:

> as if it were a given property of the mind
> that certain bounds hold against chaos.
> ("Often I Am Permitted to Return to a Meadow")

Shooting Flares into the Future

Imagine that you are going somewhere toward an event —maybe a meeting or a date, or a test, or a party. You don't know what will happen there, you *can't* know that. Yet even as you walk or drive toward the encounter, if you pay careful attention, you will almost certainly discover that your mind is spontaneously generating images of the upcoming event. Sometimes they are just still scenes, like colored slides flashed on a mental screen; sometimes they are elaborate scenarios or fantasies that briefly zip through your consciousness. Maybe an image of someone you expect to see there, or of the physical layout of the place itself. Perhaps a fantasy of yourself easefully triumphing, although sometimes we are as likely to imagine ourselves goofing up or blundering. It's not the specific content of these imagined scenes or images that matters, but their mere existence. They are like the phosphorous flares that foxholed soldiers used to fire out into the night to illuminate the landscape and perhaps tell them where the enemy was located. They are the imagination's attempt to populate the blankness of the Unknowable Next so as to reassure the self and allay its anxiety about what could happen in the future.

It's perfectly natural for these images and scenarios to occur. In fact, that's my point: it's how the mind works, or at least one of the important ways the mind works as it copes with an awareness of disorder and our need for reassurance. As we move through our daily tasks, our minds (or imaginations) are constantly sending up similar images, scenarios, and fantasies—most of them so mundane and brief we don't even pay any attention to them. But they have enormous survival value because they allow us to anticipate possibilities and options and thus help us to move forward into the unknown without too much disabling anxiety.

Making Sense of the Vanished Past

"And in my memory too I meet myself."
ST. AUGUSTINE, *Confessions*

Not only do we use imagination to produce scenarios and images to flash on the blank screen of the future, we also use imagination to order our past. The best illustration of this is provided by personal memories, especially those we cherish from childhood or youth. Any courtroom lawyer can tell us that human memory is extremely fallible and that the vivid accounts of even the most alert eyewitnesses are riddled with errors and inaccuracies. How many of us have compared our own memory of a past family event with that of a sibling or parent who was there, only to discover that our recollection of facts and the sequence of events differs drastically from theirs, not to mention the crucial detail emphasized in one recollection and completely missing from the other—"But what about what Aunt Louise did next!? Surely you can't have forgotten that!" Or we will put together two separate childhood homes to form a memory of a single place—"No, no," our mother says, "that park was near the other house where we lived when you were six." If childhood memories aren't accurate storage of information, then what are they?

They are several important things. For one thing, they are stories—coherent acts of ordering imagination. What kind of stories? Stories in which we have arranged and rearranged the details, events, sequences, and characters in such a way as to tell, in a kind of code, *how* we felt about something or someone in our past. The child's memory of the dangerously weird Uncle Al may not be factually accurate (according to adults), but it is an extremely accurate story of the child's feelings or intuitions about Al. And the parents' attempt to convince the child that the memory is "wrong" misses the point entirely. Why? Because the child's memory is his or her attempt to make sense out of the disturbing disorder Uncle Al embodied. Our personal memories, especially those from our earliest years, tell us important things about our feelings and attitudes toward the world and the people we encountered in it.

Story, of which personal memories are an excellent example, is one of imagination's most basic ordering powers, a fundamental method of arranging the chaotic material of our experience into a form of meaning that emphasizes particular characters, specific details and actions—selected for their symbolic significance—and the ways in which these characters act or interact to reveal motive and character. What's more, these stories called personal memory are crucial to our sense of self.

The loss of all personal memories is often one of the most poignant consequences of amnesia and can lead the patient to a deep sense of despair—because *who* we feel ourselves to be is largely a matter of personal memory: a collection of stories by which we explain, to ourselves and others, where we came from, what forces formed us, and who we are. Without our personal memories, we fall victim entirely to the terror of the Vanished Past. Memories of those things and people we love are cherished all the more because of the ceaseless vanishing that characterizes our life in time. To cling, in memory, to what we loved is to give more substance to our own ephemeral existence.

Let me give two more examples of the way in which the story-making imagination functions to order the disorder of the past. I'll call the first a "victim story." Someone has had a car accident or been the victim of a mugging on a dark street. Something happened that was violent and unpredictable, against which we were essentially powerless. One way or another that kind of thing has happened to almost all of us or someone we know well.

And yet, a peculiar things happens within a short time after the incident, as the victim begins trying to make sense of the experience.

That effort is likely to take the form of constructing a version of the event (a story) that often goes something like this: "I *knew* I shouldn't have gone down that street . . ." or "I *had* to have seen that car coming from the side, and if only I'd swerved left instead of going straight . . ." As the victim reexperiences the traumatic event by retelling it, he or she often creates a story that features an "I" who had, or almost had, control over what happened. Listening to the person as they try to create a persuasive story of their role in the experience, we often have an uneasy feeling. After all, to an uninvolved observer what took place has a lot to do with random bad luck—a simple matter of being in the wrong place at the wrong moment, when forces beyond our control impinged on our lives. But we humans are unable to bear the notion of our powerlessness against random violence, and story-making, no matter how unrealistic the story, becomes a major ally in preserving our sense of control over our destiny and circumstances.

An even more extreme instance of stories constructed by victims occurs sometimes in spousal abuse situations. How often police and medical authorities listen with dismay to a victim's account of her injuries at the hands of an abusing spouse. What the authorities want is for the victim to say, "He did this to me." But what they frequently hear is an account that goes like this: "It wasn't really his fault. I made him angry and when he gets angry he does this." Such a version of the event appalls the listeners' sense of morality and reality, but it is yet another example of how the individual self has a deep need to feel that it is in control of even the most violent disorders that assail it. It does no good to say, "This story is nonsense; this isn't right or true." The victim's self is struggling to survive by making a story in which it has some control over its fate. And it's very difficult to intervene in this order-making process and help the victim to construct a different story, because that different story would necessarily emphasize the extreme and dangerous vulnerability of the self, which is harder to bear by far.

In a victim story, the self is implausibly asserted to be in control in a crisis, and disorder is thus held at bay. In a "blame story," the self makes up or subscribes to a story in which the disorder afflicting the self is "really" not random or accidental, but the result consciously intended by a powerful individual or group. Here again, the disorder is tamed, is shown to be only *apparently* chaotic, but actually/secretly under the control of the conspirator or villain. When the self says, "*You* did this to me," there is a paradoxical sense in which the speaker is still in control, is still constructing the story that explains what happened (even if the story seems to be about how the self was hurt or exploited).

Conspiracy theories are variants on the blame story. Instead of being the result of impersonal and unpredictable forces, a disaster is said to be caused by a small, secret group who control and intend these dire events. Conspiracy theories in general are narratives whose seductive story lines explain why the individual self (the teller) is powerless. The *content* of such a blame story is the triumph of destructive disorder, but the *form* of the blame is narrative ordering in which someone is still in control. What's more, by being "in the know" about the conspiracy, the devotee of conspiracy theories has an added edge of control—they have the power and knowledge to tell the "true" story.

All of us, from time to time, construct blame stories in our personal and social lives. They are a mental strategy for relieving our anxiety about the random forces that seem to move through the universe like a wild wind.

My point isn't about right or wrong, or about the accuracy of victim stories or blame stories, but about the power of storytelling itself: how it gives the self/storyteller a sense that he or she is able to order disorder and violence and make sense of it. "Any sorrow can be borne if it can be made into a story, or if a story can be told about it," wrote Isak Dinesen, the Danish author of *Out of Africa*. No quote I know more perfectly expresses the survival function of story-making: it helps us to live.

From Life to Lyric Poetry

> When the two met, they both sat down to have a cry
> together. Rehua cried simple but Tane cried with a
> meaning, in verses.
> "The Mythology and Traditions of the Maori in New Zealand"

Our daily consciousness is an endless, often half-conscious interplay of our awareness of disorder and our need for order. By and large we manage to function in this way, doing our best to anticipate the future with little images and scenarios or even full-blown fantasies and ordering important aspects of our past into the story forms of personal memory. But what does this have to do with poetry? In poetry, the terms of our lives are transformed into language. But what kind of language and for what purpose?

There are, of course, many purposes for turning life into language, but my concern here is a particular literary form I'll call the personal lyric. By personal lyric, I mean a poem that usually features an "I" and that focuses on autobiographical experience or a personal crisis of some sort. At some point in prehistory, human culture developed the personal lyric so that imagination would have another way of assisting the individual self to cope. When someone, in the throes of a powerful and disturbing experience, turns instinctively to the writing or reading of a poem, it is because they sense the personal lyric can be a powerful aid in helping them survive and make sense of their experience.

In the personal lyric, the self encounters its existential crises in symbolic form, and the poem that results is a model of this encounter. By making such a dramatized, expressive model of its crisis, the self is able to acknowledge the existence, nature, and power of what is destabilizing it, while at the same time asserting its ultimate mastery over the disordering by the power of its linguistic and imaginative orderings.

Such a poem isn't meant to simplistically turn disorder into order or chaos into cosmos. Poetic order is not a cookie cutter, and existential disorder is not pastry dough—you can't just press down with a sonnet cookie-cutter in the shape of a gingerbread man or a star. In lyric poetry, disorder is *dynamic*.

CHAPTER TWO

The Dinner Party and the Sailor at War

A surprising number of scholars and teachers and even poets—people who claim to "know" what poetry is—will insist that only one aspect of poetry is crucial. Insist for instance, that the essence of poetry is formal coherence (order) or that only emotion matters (disorder). Maybe this one-sided emphasis is a temperamental thing. For some people, the need for order is so pronounced and pleasurable that order seems everything to them in the project of poetry. And for others, the destabilizing claims or threats of experience are so urgent that it would be impossible for them to talk about poetry without emphasizing passion. We see a variation on this unresolvable struggle in many of the arguments about whether free verse or formal poetry is more legitimate. For free-verse adherents, rhythm is subservient to the unique expressive dictates of the individual poetic urge behind the poem; for formalist poets, rhythm is to be regularized into the structural ordering of meter, which is in turn declared to be an essential element of poetry. Both sides are committed to the overall orderings of poetry, but in their attitudes toward the element of rhythm (or meter), they reveal their temperamental bias toward disorder (free verse) or order (formalism).

Finally, whether the emphasis is on poetry's order or disorder depends on the needs or desires of the particular poet (or reader). And it's possible that the same poet might feel differently at different times. Consider the following two anecdotes by the *same* poet about how young poets first begin to write and what function it has in their lives.

In the first anecdote, Richard Wilbur, one of our finest contemporary formalist poets, predictably stresses a serene initiation process by which a series of young artists is inspired to imitate older, established monuments of artistic order in their respective art forms:

> I remember a dinner party at a house in Cambridge, years ago. Almost everyone at the table that evening could be considered some sort of an artist, and it occurred to our host to suggest that we all testify, in turn, as to how we had first felt the call to practice one art or another. To tell the truth, I have forgotten most of the testimony, but I do recall what kind of thing was said. The novelist, let's suppose, had come across a set of Trollope in a summerhouse; the composer had heard Caruso on the gramophone, or an organist practicing Bach in an empty church; the portrait painter, perhaps, had gone with his mother to call on Mr. Sargent in his studio. It was all like that. Not one of the deponents had anything to say about the turmoil of first love, the song of the thrush, or the Bay of Naples. What had started them off as artists, they said, were no such approved stimuli, but the encounter with art itself. Astonished by a poem, a painting, a fugue, they had wanted to make something like *that*. ("Poetry's Debt to Poetry," 1972)

I should confess immediately that, in order to react with interest to the above anecdote, I have to put aside my own social biases. I am almost as uncomfortable reading about this elite gathering and its smug dismissal of emotions as I would be if I were actually sitting at the table and trying to remember which fork to use with the salad course. But I want to put that prejudice of mine aside because if I yield to it, I'll miss what Wilbur is saying. I take Wilbur to mean that one way that first poems get written is through astonishment at the achieved order of someone else's poem and the sudden desire to imitate this wondrous thing, to "make something like that." And certainly, when anyone begins writing a poem, he or she has, stored away in the mental attic somewhere, a model of what a poem is. If you are young and naive, the model is whatever you once read as a poem that mattered to you (it could be Shelley or Frost, or it could be something from a greeting card). Not all first-time artists hear Bach in a church or visit John Singer Sargent's studio—not all of us have our first encounter with achieved form at such a sophisticated level—but Wilbur's point remains well taken.

And yet, there's a funny silence in the middle of the dinner chatter. Wilbur himself doesn't say how *he* began writing. Since it took place "years ago," he's forced to make up even his fellow guests' origin stories ("To tell the truth, I have forgotten most of the testimony . . ."), but surely he might have added his own testimony, which presumably would have paralleled and reinforced that of his fellow diners.

It so happens that we *do* have a brief passage from another Wilbur essay, where he is more candid about his own background and the circumstances under which he first began writing. As a young man, Wilbur served in the U.S. Navy during the Second World War as a sailor aboard a destroyer escorting convoys across the U-boat–haunted Atlantic. Such a hazardous experience places him far from the unanguished comforts of Cambridge dinner parties, and sure enough, this succinct story has a very different emphasis: "My first poems were written in answer to the inner and outer disorders of the Second World War and they helped me, as poems should, to take ahold of raw events and convert them, provisionally, into experience" ("On My Own Work," 1966). In this single sentence we have the turmoil of youth and the uncertainties and perils of war—the "inner and outer disorders"—presented as the instigators of his "first poems." We see here how dynamic disorder initiates an ordering response ("in answer to") and also how that ordering has therapeutic power against that disorder ("helped me . . . to take ahold of").

Neither story is the "true" story of how Richard Wilbur thinks poetry begins; or, rather, both stories are true. They differ in that the first story stresses artistic order as a triumph in its own right, something sought for its pure pleasure quality, while the second story stresses the urgent, destabilizing disorder of experience as the initiating motive force behind poem-making.

IT WOULD BE impossible to speculate meaningfully on Wilbur's reticence about his wartime initiation into poem making, but certainly such an anecdote would have struck a jarring note at the dinner party. I remember vividly my own sense of what I can only call shame when, after several years of apprenticeship, I realized that I *needed* desperately to write about my brother's and mother's deaths. At the time, I thought of poetry as a citadel of purity whose high, shining walls were designed expressly to keep out topics so saturated with human misery. I even thought if I could somehow get inside those walls, I might be safe from my suffering. No one told me that poetry could be an open forge where I could bring the raw material of my life to be fashioned into poems. Such a discovery, such a granting of permission to use your own life experience in poetry can be tremendously important. Here is the contemporary poet Dorianne Laux recounting her first time in a poetry workshop:

> I was in my late twenties, a single mother, working as a waitress at a small family restaurant. . . . I had been told to write about what I knew, and what I knew was my life, a life I wasn't sure was acceptable as subject matter for poetry, a life that included instances of domestic violence and sexual abuse. In Steve's workshop I was given permission to write about that life. I was working class. I was a woman. I was a mother. Could this mundane, ordinary world be a subject for my poetry? (foreword to *In the Palm of Your Hand*, by Steven Kowit)

In my own apprenticeship, Stanley Kunitz's "The Portrait," a poem concerning his father's suicide, changed my notion of what a poem might be. His poem showed me that something lucid and wonderful could be made out of dismaying personal material, and it gave me hope that I, too, might bring language and shaping imagination to bear on the specific and agonized circumstances of my own adolescence.

Culture's Other Gifts: Religion and Philosophy

> However, rational cognition has one critical limit which is
> its inability to cope with suffering. Reason can subsume
> suffering under concepts; it can furnish means to alleviate
> suffering; but it can never express suffering in the medium
> of experience, for to do so would be irrational by reason's
> own standards.
>
> THEODOR ADORNO, *Aesthetic Theory*

I've spoken of the personal lyric as a "gift," given since time immemorial to members of a culture to help them survive individual existential crises. Culture has, of course, given other gifts that also propose survival strategies, religion and philosophy chief among them.

Typically, in both religion and philosophy the self is assisted by being subsumed into a larger order, either abstract and conceptual in philosophy or sacred and divine in religion. Religion tends to postulate heaven or its equivalent as an alternate world, or stipulates that the soul is an immortal, detachable aspect of our being, and thus sets up the terms by which the self can shed its material suffering and flee or anticipate fleeing to a peaceful haven. Or it asserts that there is a cosmic, sacred order at work in the world and, if we trust that divine order rather than our own, necessarily limited perspective, we will be released from our burden of misery and confusion (for a more extended discussion of the differences between religion and poetry, see appendix A). Philosophy sets up reason as an opposite of emotion and says: we must be reasonable, not emotional, if we are to get through this crisis. In doing so, philosophy has asked us to abandon a central aspect of the self: its subjectivity.

Plato, the founder of Western idealist philosophy, polarized the distinction between lyrical and philosophical approaches. Referring to some "ancient quarrel between poetry and philosophy," Plato claimed poetry emerged from and appealed to the emotional aspect of the human soul and was thus tainted with a dangerous and self-defeating irrationality. He insisted that only reason and logic could make us happy and orderly, going so far as to urge an ideal city-state society from which all poets would be banned on pain of death: "For if you grant admission to the honeyed Muse in lyric or epic, pleasure and pain will be lords of your city, instead of law" (*Republic*, book X). Rather than letting the self be ruled by its "weak" subjectivity, Plato counseled detaching the rational aspect of the soul from its irrational, emotional aspect, identifying with the rational while suppressing the irrational. We owe an enormous debt to Plato's project for establishing and clarifying such abstract, ideal principles as "truth" and "justice," which the self can use to orient and regulate its behavior. But the personal lyric cries out that pain and pleasure *are* powerful and central realities of human being and subjectivity *is* a central truth that needs to be accommodated, needs to be included in the story and regulated through expression, not suppression.

What distinguishes the personal lyric from philosophy and religion is that the personal lyric *clings to embodied being*. Wordsworth praises this as poetry's fidelity to "sensuous incarnation," a holding-close to the individual and the details of his or her world. The personal lyric says to the self in its suffering: "I will not abandon you. Nor will I ask you to abandon yourself and the felt truth and particulars of your experience."

Rather than the transcendence counseled by philosophy and religion, the personal lyric urges the self to *translate* its whole being into language where it can dramatize and restabilize itself in the patterned language of the poem. The personal lyric takes the physical terms of human crisis (the characters, the setting, the sensations) and brings them over into language: it takes body and makes it "body," takes tulips and makes them "tulips." Takes the self and makes it "I." Takes another self and makes it "you" or "she" or "he."

Translating the World and the Body

> Language is a skin. I rub my language against the other.
> It is as if I had words instead of fingers, or fingers at the tip
> of my words.
>
> ROLAND BARTHES, *A Lover's Discourse*

When God, in the Hebraic account of creation, had finished making all the things in the world, he brought them one by one before Adam, and Adam gave them names. This naming of the birds and beasts gave Adam "dominion." His ability to attach language to the animals was a form of power over them. To name something is to begin to assert control over it. Conversely, in the classic horror tales of Poe or H. P. Lovecraft, one way of signaling the protagonist's powerlessness was to say that he was confronted by a "nameless horror."

Helen Keller, who became blind and deaf before the age of nineteen months, has left an account of how she first learned language. As anyone who has seen *The Miracle Worker* or read Keller's autobiography recalls, Keller was a violent and unruly child. We can only imagine how terrifying it was to be her—living entirely surrounded by an eerily silent blackness, unable to communicate with anyone. Here is her account of the moment that transformed her life forever—her discovery of language at the age of seven:

> We walked down the path to the well-house, attracted by the fragrance of the honeysuckle with which it was covered. Someone was drawing water and my teacher placed my hand under the spout. As the cool stream gushed over my hand she spelled into the other the word *water*, first slowly, then rapidly. I stood still, my whole attention fixed upon the motion of her fingers. Suddenly I felt a misty consciousness as of something forgotten—a thrill of returning thought; and somehow the mystery of language was revealed to me. I knew then that w-a-t-e-r meant the wonderful cool something that was flowing over my hand. That living word awakened my soul, gave it light, hope, joy, set it free! (Helen Keller, *The Story of My Life*, 1902)

A little later, she becomes aware of how language connects her to the world of things: "I did nothing but explore with my hands and learn the name of every object that I touched; and the more I handled things and learned their names and uses, the more joyous and confident grew my sense of kinship with the rest of the world." What joy Keller feels as she connects language and sensory experience of the world and begins to realize that she can orient herself in her dark, silent world through words—that language itself is a form of sight.

HELEN KELLER is not the only one to relish the power of concrete nouns to create a sense of connection between self and world. The contemporary German poet Günter Eich found himself struggling to write a sustaining poetry in the aftermath of World War II, when the cultural and physical landscape of Germany had been devastated and partially obliterated by years of warfare and by the recent Allied bombardments. For Eich, the first and essential step was to create or recreate a solid world to inhabit, and he did so by writing a poetry made up primarily of nouns, or "thing-words" as they are called in German. Here are some excerpts from Eich's 1956 talk, "Some Remarks about Literature and Reality":

> I write poems to orient myself in reality. I view them as trigonometric points or buoys that mark the course in an unknown area. Only through writing do things take on reality for me. Reality is my goal, not my presupposition. First I must establish it. . . .
>
> I am a writer. Writing is not only a profession but also a decision to see the world as language. Real language is a falling together of the word and the object. Our task is to translate from the language that is around us but not "given. . . ."
>
> I must admit that I have not come very far along in this translating. I still am not beyond the "thing-word" or noun. I am like a child who says "tree," "moon," "mountain" and thus orients himself.

LANGUAGE, ESPECIALLY the language of concrete nouns and sensations, may be the hand of imagination with which we touch the world. But language is not limited to its ability to connect us with the objects that surround us in the world. We have a language for feeling states also. When I say "I am sad," I connect an emotion to a word, and thus an inner state is given the objective and social existence of language. Such an act of self-definition and self-dramatization allows me to connect with my own subjectivity and clarify it to myself. And such language also allows me to externalize my subjective state and dramatize it to others, connecting me to their world as surely as the word "water" connects me to something in the world of objects.

The Thread of Language

> Now it appears to me that almost any Man may like the spider spin from his own inwards his own airy Citadel—the points of leaves and twigs on which the spider begins her work are few, and she fills the air with a beautiful circuiting.
> JOHN KEATS, letter of Feb. 19, 1818

When Wordsworth claims that the poet carries "everywhere with him relationship and love," he is speaking of the eros quality inherent in the project of writing the lyric poem: the life-urge to connect. *Eros*, the Greek word for love, is what connects the "I" of the personal lyric to the other words of the poem and the words of the poem to the world itself. Likewise, eros is what connects the self to the inner world of its own feelings and to the outer world of objects, animals, and other people. Eros is the affirmation of the human spirit as life-force.

Keats begins his early long poem "Endymion" with this famous claim:

> A thing of beauty is a joy forever:
> Its loveliness increases; it will never
> Pass into nothingness.

According to Keats, something that is beautiful doesn't perish, and this "fact" becomes the basic motive for creativity, the making of things:

Therefore, on every morrow, are we wreathing
A flowery band to bind us to the earth. (ll. 6–7)

The process of making beautiful things (say, poems) is imaged as
the making of a rope of flowers whose purpose is to hold us to the
material world—as though, without such a tether, the self would
float away, utterly detached. This "flowery band" is, among other
things, an image for the rhythmical energy of a line of poetry. The
eros of language imaged as fragrant entanglements.

Walt Whitman has yet another image for the way that the eros of
language links the self to the sensory world:

A noiseless patient spider,
I mark'd where on a little promontory it stood isolated,
Mark'd how to explore the vacant vast surrounding
It launch'd forth filament, filament, filament, out of itself,
Ever unreeling them, ever tirelessly speeding them.

And you O my soul where you stand,
Surrounded, detached, in measureless oceans of space,
Ceaselessly musing, venturing, throwing, seeking the spheres, to
    connect them,
Till the bridge you will need be form'd, till the ductile anchor hold,
Till the gossamer thread you fling catch somewhere, O my soul.
(1891–92 edition)

Early draft lines of this poem, from 1863, show even more clearly that
the spider is a symbol for the human self seeking eros connections:

The soul, reaching throwing out for *love*,
As the spider, from some little promontory,
        throwing out filament after filament,
tirelessly out of itself, that one at
least may catch and form a link,
a bridge, a connection.

Without the spider filament of language, the flowery band that binds us to the earth, the self is isolated, cut off from the surrounding world.

Solitude and the Forlorn

Aloneness is an existential condition. We are born alone; we die alone. I live alone inside the world of my body in the sense that no one feels or can feel exactly what I feel, because he or she exists in the separate and distinct world of his or her own body.

When we can feel this existential aloneness as a kind of stability, even a pleasure, we call it solitude. The Romantic poets, who taught us the pleasure of long walks in nature, also taught us that solitude can be an opportunity to renew one's powers by withdrawing into the self.

But when we experience our aloneness negatively, we might use another term that also came into vogue with the first Romantics: "forlorn." When the self is forlorn, it feels its aloneness as anguish, as being cut off from eros, from connectedness. William Wordsworth devoted numerous lines and poems to the joys of solitude, but he stresses the word "forlorn" in the following sonnet about the self alienated from the natural world through too much preoccupation with "getting and spending":

The World Is Too Much with Us

The world is too much with us; late and soon,
Getting and spending, we lay waste our powers:
Little we see in Nature that is ours;
We have given our hearts away, a sordid boon!
This Sea that bares her bosom to the moon;
The winds that will be howling at all hours,
And are up-gathered now like sleeping flowers;
For this, for every thing, we are out of tune;
It moves us not.—Great God! I'd rather be
A Pagan suckled in a creed outworn;
So might I, standing on this pleasant lea,

Have glimpses that would make me less forlorn;
Have sight of Proteus rising from the sea;
Or hear old Triton blow his wreathed horn.

Nor is disconnection from the natural world and its pleasures the only cause of forlornness. In the next sonnet, written after his beloved daughter's death, Wordsworth dramatizes the devastating distance between shared intimacy and anguished aloneness by focusing on the brief moment of lines one and two in which he has momentarily forgotten his loss, only to have the knowledge of it return with crushing force in line three:

Surprised by Joy

Surprised by joy—impatient as the Wind
I turned to share the transport—Oh! with whom
But Thee, deep buried in the silent tomb,
That spot which no vicissitude can find?
Love, faithful love, recalled thee to my mind—
But how could I forget thee? Through what power,
Even for the least division of an hour,
Have I been so beguiled as to be blind
To my most grievous loss!—That thought's return
Was the worst pang that sorrow ever bore,
Save one, one only, when I stood forlorn,
Knowing my heart's best treasure was no more;
That neither present time, nor years unborn
Could to my sight that heavenly face restore.

To be forlorn is to feel one's self in the grip of *thanatos*, the Greek word for death and the contrary of eros. But to suffer the anguish of isolation and alienation is far better than not to feel at all. To be forlorn is to confront a powerful existential disorder, and it can call up powerful orderings as well. In "The World Is Too Much with Us," the vision of the pagan gods is held out as a possibility of wonder and awe to offset alienation. "Surprised by Joy" is a far more somber encounter—not only grief but guilt at momentarily forgetting his grief assails the speaker, and against this there is no thematic affirmation possible, only the formal ordering of the rhymed sonnet to brace the wretched self against its losses. Still, even this sorrow has been borne. It has, as Isak Dinesen would say, been made into a story.

CHAPTER THREE

The Embodied Self

All thoughts and actions emanate from the body. . . .
Through my small, bonebound island I have learnt all
I know, experienced all, and sensed all. All I write is
inseparable from the island. As much as possible, therefore,
I employ the scenery of the island to describe the scenery
of my thoughts, the earthquakes of the body to describe
the earthquakes of the heart.

The Notebooks of Dylan Thomas

In order to carry the weight of the existential crises that torment it from without and within, the self in the personal lyric needs to be more than a stick figure "I." It's a pronoun whose formidable task is to incarnate and dramatize a full range of human feelings, thoughts, memories, and sensations even as it faces the past and the present or anticipates the future.

Freud tells us that the ego is "first and foremost a body Ego," and D. H. Lawrence has provided a vivid evocation of this complicated embodiment:

Why should I look at my hand, as it so cleverly writes these words, and decide that it is a mere nothing compared to the mind that directs it? Is there really any huge difference between my hand and my brain? Or my mind? My hand is alive, it flickers with a life of its own. It meets all the strange universe in touch, and learns a vast number of things, and knows a vast number of things. My hand, as it writes these words, slips gaily along, jumps like a grasshopper to dot an *i*, feels the table rather cold, gets a little bored if I write too long, has its own rudiments of thought, and is just as much *me* as is my brain, my mind, or my soul. Why should I imagine that there is a *me*, which is more me than my hand is? Since my hand is absolutely alive, me alive.

Whereas, of course, as far as I am concerned, my pen isn't alive at all. My pen *isn't* me alive. Me alive ends at my finger-tips.

Whatever is me alive is me. ("Why the Novel Matters")

Lawrence's "me alive," with all its awareness of the world, becomes collapsed into the pronoun "I" in language. But that small word "I" is like the narrow passage for sand in an hourglass: on the far side of it there is an opening up to the marvelous richness of consciousness.

Howard Gardner, a Harvard developmental psychologist, offers this definition of "self" in his book *Frames of Mind*. Self, he says, is "an invented figure of speech—a fictional entity of the mind." One that is useful in taking "the inchoate understanding that lies at the core of intrapersonal intelligence and making it public (via symbol systems) and accessible to the person themself (and to others as well)." These symbol systems, especially language, allow the individual to create his or her self—the invented figure of speech—and that self, in turn, is a "model of what that person is like, what he has done, what his strengths and weaknesses are, how he feels about himself, etc." (295).

If Lawrence's evocation stresses the body nature of self, then Gardner's indicates how the self makes use of language to create and orient itself both internally and in terms of other selves in the social world.

Self-Centered and the Self as Center

What a history is folded, folded inward and inward
again in the single word "I."
WALT WHITMAN, *Day Books and Notebooks*

The personal lyric is "self-centered" not in the sense of conceited but in the sense that the me-alive, embodied self is the nexus of our most important experiences, indeed, of all our experiences. Thus Thoreau, in the opening paragraphs of *Walden*, tells us his book will be like any other book we've ever read except that we'll hear the word "I" a lot—but from whom else but the self can we get our essential, existential knowledge? "In most books, the I, or first person, is omitted; in this it will be retained; that, in respect to egotism, is the main difference. We commonly do not remember that it is, after all, always the first person that is speaking. I should not talk so much about myself if there were *any body* else whom I knew as well" (1, my italics). Note that he says "any body"—that it's not a single word, "anybody," but two words that, in their separateness, heighten our awareness that "I," "self," and "body" form an essential cluster of meaning and knowledge.

In order for a personal lyric to come into being, the speaker, the "I" of the poem, must momentarily but absolutely believe that he or she is the central point around which all meaning constellates. Of course, such a belief would make a person insufferable if he or she lived an entire life exclusively according to this principle. But we are talking here of the conditions in which a personal lyric is born—a crisis of the spirit, not a relentless, daily egotism. The great twentieth-century Spanish poet Antonio Machado addresses the danger of a poet's failure to invest commitment and imaginative confidence in the centrality of self: "When the poet doubts that the center of the universe lies in his own heart, that his spirit is an overflowing fountain, a focus which irradiates creative energy capable of informing and even of deforming the world around him, then the spirit of the poet wanders disoriented again among objects" (quoted in *The Poet's Work*, 164).

Subjectivity

One does not begin by reasoning but by feeling.
JEAN-JACQUES ROUSSEAU (1759)

The lyric poet . . . sings not some objective thing before
which he sacrifices his subjective individuality, but his very
subjectivity itself.
G. W. F. HEGEL (1828)

The centrality of the self to lyric ordering brings us to
one of the main questions about lyric poetry: can it handle the flux
and chaos of feeling? A number of the Romantic and pre-Romantic
philosophers and poets who championed the personal lyric in the
West were optimistic. Here's William Blake, who seems to feel that
all we need to do is acknowledge that the roller coaster of emotional
highs and lows is our human destiny:

It is right it should be so;
Man was made for Joy & Woe;
And when this we rightly know
Thro' the World we safely go.
("Auguries of Innocence")

According to the logic of Blake's lines our task is to come to terms
with the fact that we are feeling creatures, creatures of our feelings.
It's true that many of the forces that disorder our lives exist objectively and are external to the self, such as poverty, war, loss of a loved
one. Yet as Emily Dickinson notes, the disordering may start as far
outside the body self as an angle of light across a landscape, but it
is only when and how it registers within us that it comes to matter
and mean:

There's a certain Slant of light,
Winter Afternoons –
That oppresses, like the Heft
Of Cathedral Tunes –

Heavenly Hurt, it gives us –
We can find no scar,
But internal difference,
Where the Meanings, are – (J. 258)

Nor is it always an easy matter to say what is external and what is internal to the self. When someone I love dies, his death, his ceasing to exist as a biological entity is objective. It's a fact in a world of facts. But what that person's death *means* for me involves an enormously complex and confusing tangle of emotions, thoughts, sensations, memories, and imaginings. Involves, in short, my subjectivity.

Likewise, when we fall passionately in love with someone, when we suddenly become possessed by intense desire for a person, that person exists objectively in the world, but *how* that person makes us feel is the important issue. And that delirious confabulation places us, once again, deep in the dangerous and exhilarating territory of subjectivity, where disorder is the order of the day.

SUBJECTIVITY DESCRIBES US. What I *am* is subjective: I am this embodied self that feels, thinks, senses, remembers, imagines. And all in a dizzying swirl, and with the inner radio going all the time. But it may be that this mildly chaotic state is just the day-to-day condition of our existence: who we are, what we live with and in. Until a powerful crisis destabilizes us, we may not even realize how precarious an entity that self really is. And it's then that the personal lyric steps forward with its offer to restabilize us. What was buzz and din becomes an "I" whose actions and articulations express and regulate the confusions of our situation.

Now there shall be a man cohered out of tumult and chaos.
WHITMAN, 1855 preface to *Leaves of Grass*

In his essay "The Poet," Emerson tells us "a man is only half himself; the other half is his expression." Who we are, our inner life, is not only confusing to us but also a mystery to others. In a somber mood, Chekhov remarked, "The soul of another is wrapped in darkness." In a less grim state of mind, the sixth Dalai Lama, a seventeenth-century Tibetan religious leader who also wrote sensuous love poems, had a similar perception about the inaccessibility of another's subjectivity:

> Drawing diagrams I measured
> Movements of the stars;
> Though her tender flesh is near
> Her mind I cannot measure.

The personal lyric orders and dramatizes our subjectivity and externalizes it as language. One burden the self commonly carries is that we are cut off from other people, isolated by our subjectivity. Through the personal lyric, a self can dramatize its situation and enter the shared world of language and connection to other selves.

IN THE EARLY history of the West, as far as the dominant culture was concerned, the personal lyric was a minor form of literature, and neither the ancient Greek nor Roman critics had much to say about it. Given that, in the West, we commonly assume that the concept of the importance of the individual was invented and enshrined in our part of the globe and that lyric poetry is the expression of individual feeling, such a dearth of critical attention to the lyric might seem odd. However, our main Western conceptions of the individual derive from Plato and Aristotle. The former's insistence on rationality and the latter's emphasis on man as a social and political creature caused them both to distrust and denigrate the emotional dimension of the self that is central to lyric expression. In China and Japan on the other hand, the lyric has been the central expression of literary culture for thousands of years, and innumerable critics have given their theories and opinions about it. For instance, here is the sixth-century Chinese critic Liu Hsieh, in *The Literary Mind and the Carving of Dragons*, his famous treatise on poetry: "It is the expression of the five emotions which gives the essence of literature." (In China, these "five emotions" were joy, anger, sadness, pleasure, and resentment.) And again: "The main purpose (of literary writing) is to express inner feeling."

Liu Hsieh even uses an image of weaving to present something very similar to my definition of poetry as the interplay of disorder and order: "Emotion is the warp of literary pattern, linguistic form the woof of ideas. Only when the warp is straight can the woof be rightly formed, and only when ideas are definite can linguistic form be meaningful."

The Three Strange Angels

There's a proverb that shows up in many cultures and goes something like this: the willow that bends in the wind survives; the oak that resists, breaks. The wisdom that underlies the personal lyric is akin to this proverb. This wisdom says: the way to survive disorder is to let it enter you, to open yourself to it, rather than resisting it or denying its power and presence. For me, the poem that best dramatizes that wisdom is a poem by D. H. Lawrence called "Song of a Man Who Has Come Through" (1914). It's an oddly complicated poem, and I don't want to do more than sketch the way its early lines unfold, because it is only in the final five lines that I find the deepest mystery revealed. Here's the entire poem:

Not I, not I, but the wind that blows through me!
A fine wind is blowing the new direction of Time.
If only I let it bear me, carry me, if only it carry me!
If only I am sensitive, subtle, oh, delicate, a winged gift!
If only, most lovely of all, I yield myself and am borrowed
By the fine, fine wind that takes its course through the chaos of the
    world
Like a fine, an exquisite chisel, a wedge-blade inserted;
If only I am keen and hard like the sheer tip of a wedge
Driven by invisible blows,
The rock will split, we shall come at the wonder, we shall find the
    Hesperides.

Oh, for the wonder that bubbles into my soul,
I would be a good fountain, a good well-head,
Would blur no whisper, spoil no expression.

What is the knocking?
What is the knocking at the door in the night?
It is somebody wants to do us harm.

No, no, it is the three strange angels.
Admit them, admit them.

As for the earlier part of the poem, it might be enough to say that the speaker of the poem begins with enormous incantatory confidence. The poem's title seems to indicate that he has come through some powerful though unnamed experience and emerged on the other side. But he immediately disclaims credit for his victory: it wasn't me that did it, but something larger than me—a wind that carried me. He goes on to praise the process by which one might arrive at such a place and, in the course of this praising, takes us through a series of metamorphic changes that might be necessary for such a journey. In line four, he must respond to the wind by becoming a "winged gift" almost like a wind-borne milkweed or dandelion seed, perhaps. Three lines later, he has metamorphosed into the sharp tip of a chisel, and the wind itself is the chisel. He imagines breaking apart a rock and releasing what was hidden inside it: the "wonder," which is like a gushing spring, or even that garden of the gods where, according to the ancient Greeks, golden apples grew that were guarded by four nymphs known as the Hesperides. The exhilarated speaker goes on to avow his desire to *be* that spring or fountain and articulate what he experienced. And then we arrive at the abrupt, odd shift of the poem's last five lines.

The confident (even boasting) speaker of stanza two is startled by the "knocking" of stanza three. Immediately, his attitude and tone change. There is a knock at the door (and with those words, we seem suddenly and inexplicably to be inside some dwelling at night), and he is seized with fear: "It is somebody wants to do us harm." Then, in the poem's final two-line stanza, it's as if another voice, or perhaps the voice of some other part of him, answers his fear: "No, no, it is the three strange angels. / Admit them, admit them."

Who are these three strange angels whose sudden appearance has so completely unnerved our speaker? I don't think we can know. There are three of them, which is a magical number whether one thinks of the mystic Christian trinity of Father, Son, and Holy Ghost or the triple forms of the ancient goddess Hecate or the three Graces, or the three Fates, or any number of other magical or supernatural figures who appear in groups of three. The Hesperides mentioned earlier are the four daughters of Night who, in Greek myth, guard the golden apples, and in some tellings there are three rather than four, but they are never "angels." If the Bible or Torah is part of our heritage, we might think of the "three men" who appear outside Abraham's tent in Genesis 18 to tell him that his aged wife Sarah will bear a child. Still, these possible allusions don't give us any "answer" (as if the poem were a question, which it isn't). They only bring us back to what the poem tells us: they are angels. "Angel" comes from the Greek for "messenger." We can go on to say that being angels means that they are powerful, even magical beings of a mostly benevolent nature. I say "mostly" benevolent because the adjective "strange" might rightly make us a little nervous about their nature. If the poem said simply, "It is the three angels," we would have less to ponder. But the half rhyme of "strange angels" fuses the two words into a single, disconcerting entity.

But it isn't just the identity of the figures that makes the poem's ending mysterious. We also note that the same someone who *knows* who is outside the door also tells us emphatically what we are to do in response to the knocking: "Admit them, admit them."

Welcoming the Angels

In each line, in each phrase the possibility of failure is concealed. The possibility that the whole poem, not just that isolated verse, will fail. That's how life is: at every moment, we can lose it. Every moment there is mortal risk.

ROBERT FROST

But why should I open the door when I hear a knock in the night? It's certainly not easy to do. Many of us have fish-eye lenses set in our doors so we can peek through and see who's out there before we open. Or a chain latch that only opens the door a crack.

It's right that we have such protections. We live in a dangerous world. Is it any different in the world of imagination? Well, we open ourselves to enormous varieties of violent disorder all the time under the guise of entertainment: action movies, horror movies, violence on television. The disorder quotient in them is very high indeed. How is that disorder different from what you might encounter in lyric poetry?

One answer is that the violence and chaos of action and horror movies is not personal—it seldom affects us deeply. On the other hand, if you hit the right lyric poem, what agitates its language will matter to you personally. It will reach you where you live. It will be knocking on *your* door and it will be *you* who has to decide whether or not to open the door and let the disorder in. With the personal lyric, if it works, there is a sense that the poem is addressing you personally. There is an intimate connection as of one person with another.

Jeopardy and excitement. Should I open the door? All my social training and cultural upbringing have told me that I should experience such a situation as a dangerous threat and adopt a defensive posture. I should resist disorder and try to dominate it. According to the mythic models that shape my response, I should take active control and subdue disorder, by heroic force, if necessary.

But the approach recommended by the personal lyric is the opposite of this: to become vulnerable, to open the door and admit the mysterious creatures who wait on our threshold seeking permission to enter. We must, the personal lyric tells us, become vulnerable to what is out there (or inside us). Not in order to be destroyed or overwhelmed by it, but as part of a strategy for dealing with it and surviving it. Lyric poetry tells us that it is precisely by letting in disorder that we will gain access to poetry's ability to help us survive. It is the initial act of surrendering to disorder that permits the ordering powers of the imagination to assert themselves.

Letting Go: Keats, Orpingalik, and Tsvetaeva

There is probably no more intriguing a version of Lawrence's advice to "admit them" than that given by Keats in a letter of 1817 to his two brothers. Keats was fascinated by Shakespeare's ability to create such various yet believable characters for his plays. How could the same, single imagination create a Hamlet and a Lear, a Macbeth and an Ophelia? Keats decided that Shakespeare's ability had less to do with a powerful and aggressive imagination or alert observation of other people than with a passive (or "negative") capability. What Shakespeare possessed more than any other writer, Keats claimed, was an ability to "let go" of his own identity and become other figures, to be a "Chameleon poet." Here's how Keats phrased it and praised it: "And at once it struck me what quality went to form a Man of Achievement, especially in Literature, and which Shakespeare possessed so enormously—I mean *Negative Capability*, that is, when a man is capable of being in uncertainties, mysteries, doubts, without any irritable reaching after fact and reason" (letter of Dec. 21, 1817). In this formulation "fact and reason" are the controlling principles the poet must hold in abeyance so as to first let in the volatile elements of mystery, uncertainty, and doubt— qualities the three strange angels are eager to haul into the house of the poem.

The jeopardy of poetry-making is deeply connected to the jeopardy of life itself. The Eskimo and Inuit peoples of the Arctic, who live in the harshest imaginable physical conditions and are intimately familiar with life's risks, have a highly developed tradition of the personal lyric. In the following description of where he felt songs came from, Orpingalik, a Netsilik Eskimo, gives another version of how the poet yields to disorder by becoming "thawed up" and "smaller," until the ordering power of imagination comes forth as a patterned song:

> Songs are thoughts sung out with the breath when people let themselves be moved by a great force and ordinary speech no longer suffices.
>
> Man is moved like an ice floe which drifts with the current. His thoughts are driven by flowing force when he feels joy, when he feels fear, when he feels sorrow. Thoughts can surge in on him, causing him to gasp for breath and making his heart beat faster. Something like a softening of the weather will keep him thawed. And then it will happen that we, who always think of ourselves as small, will feel even smaller. And we will hesitate before using words. But it will happen that the words we need will come of themselves.
>
> When the words we need shoot up of themselves—we have a new song. (recorded by Knud Rasmussen, "Report of the Fifth Thule Expedition, 1921–1924")

The great twentieth-century Russian lyric poet Marina Tsvetaeva, like Keats, also recognized the necessity for the poet to open herself to the jeopardy of disorder *before* responding with ordering power. In her phrasing, "subjection to the visitation" and "being mentally pulled to pieces" are equivalent to Lawrence's "admitting the strange angels":

> Genius: the highest degree of subjection to the visitation—one; control of visitation—two. The highest degree of being mentally pulled to pieces, and the highest of being—collected. The highest of passivity, and the highest of activity.
>
> To let oneself be annihilated right down to some last atom from the survival (resistance) of which will grow—a world. ("Art in the Light of Conscience," 1933, trans. Angela Livingstone)

Giving Form to the Inner

The poet's eye, in a fine frenzy rolling,
Doth glance from heaven to earth, from earth to heaven;
And, as imagination bodies forth
The forms of things unknown, the poet's pen
Turns them to shapes, and gives to airy nothing
A local habitation and a name.

WILLIAM SHAKESPEARE, *A Midsummer Night's Dream*

Shakespeare gives us a description of the poet giving the "airy nothings" of imagination the "shape," the "local habitation and a name" of language written out on a page. But his description is from outside. In his passage, we *see* the poet enact the process. We see him roll his eyeballs in inspired frenzy. We see him scribble away on the page. But what does it *feel* like inside the poet as he struggles to give articulation and order to the urgent and amorphous elusiveness that presses against his consciousness?

Section 50 of Whitman's "Song of Myself" is precisely such a testimony about what it feels like to yearn to give expression to the urgent formlessness within, to the subjectivity that is at the heart of lyric poetry:

There is that in me—I do not know what it is—but I know it is in me.

Wrench'd and sweaty—calm and cool then my body becomes,
I sleep—I sleep long.

I do not know it—it is without name—it is a word unsaid,
It is not in any dictionary, utterance, symbol.

Something it swings on more than the earth I swing on,
To it the creation is the friend whose embracing awakes me.

Perhaps I might tell more. Outlines! I plead for my brothers and sisters.

Do you see O my brothers and sisters?
It is not chaos or death—it is form, union, plan—it is eternal life—it is
Happiness.

Not only does Whitman express the difficulty of trying to say what is "without name," to find words for "a word unsaid" that is not in any dictionary, but he also intuits that the ordering principles, the "Outlines" of art will give it definite form. He urges us not to be afraid of the encounter with disorder: "It is not chaos or death." Whitman also makes clear his high opinion of the rewards for such an encounter: "It is form, union, plan—it is eternal life—it is Happiness."

THIS MIGHT BE a good point to draw together the testimony of our poets—which ranges from the oral traditions of Orpingalik's tribe to Shakespeare's celebratory reworking of Plato's poet as close kin to a madman—and note that they all urge an initial giving-over of the self and also endorse the poet's nimbleness and flexibility when encountering disorder. Such various yet consistent testimony suggests that "disorder" itself has multiple forms and faces. Clarity of conceptualization forces me to reduce them to a single term in order to emphasize the dynamic relationship between disorder, order, and self, but in each existential situation disorder may take a different form. It can appear as any strong passion or emotion that grips us in some circumstance or simply wells up in us. It can and does manifest itself in primal events centered around desire, death, or loss. We experience traumatic violence and suffering as disorder, but overwhelming beauty or joy can disrupt our stability as well. And the wonder and awe we feel in personal encounters with landscape or natural phenomena or phenomena that seem supernatural and numinous also testify to the various forms disorder can take as it asserts its power and presence in our lives.

CHAPTER FOUR

The Edge as Threshold

Whoever you are: at evening step forth
out of your room, where all is known to you;
last thing before the distance lies your house:
whoever you are.

RILKE, "Prelude"

In the ceaseless interplay of disorder and order in our
daily lives, it is possible (and important) to imagine that there are
certain situations where this unstable interaction can be held for a
moment in steady state. One such suspended moment is the poem,
which freeze-frames the interplay as language so that we can contemplate it, feel it, and concentrate on it. Robert Frost once characterized poetry as "a momentary stay against confusion," and his
phrase articulates with eloquent simplicity a poem's power to lift
moments of clarified drama out of the ceaseless, discombobulating
flow of experience and, by doing so, to restabilize the self.

Imagining the poem's suspended moment as a threshold between
disorder and order can tell us a lot about poetry and about ourselves.
My dictionary defines threshold as "the sill of a doorway"; "the
entrance to a house or building"; and, in psychology and physiology,
"the point where a stimulus is of sufficient intensity to produce
an effect." Taking the last definition first, we can say that in our
model of poetry, it is the disorder that "reaches sufficient intensity
to produce an effect." That effect is both a sudden awareness of
the disorder (the initiating moment of feeling destabilized) and the
imagination's ordering response to it.

But for the purposes of visualization it can be helpful to go directly to the most physical sense of threshold, that of a doorsill that is both entrance and exit to a house. As such, a threshold is a place of transition, a place where a person might pause. Imagine yourself there for a moment: you are departing and stop briefly on the threshold with the door open. Before you, the wild and varied scene of the outer world unfolds. Whether urban or pastoral, such a scene is fluid in its movements, unbounded, diverse. Behind you, available to your peripheral senses, is the interior architecture of the room you are leaving—its reassuring stability of walls, floor, and ceiling, where, as Rilke says, "all is known to you." Both directions and their implications are part of your awareness, as you pause there on the threshold. One of the most ancient gods of the Romans and Etruscans (in fact, so ancient that almost nothing was known about him) was Janus, the god of gates and entrances. Janus had two faces, one facing forward, the other backward. His head with its two faces was often carved over arches and the gates of towns and cities. Someone standing on his or her threshold is like Janus, simultaneously aware of the ordering behind them and the disorder before them.

THE SHAPE OF a doorframe also represents a powerful architecture— during earthquakes, people are advised to stand in doorways because they are stronger and safer than anyplace else in a house. It's possible to imagine the rectangle of a doorway as the rectangular shape of the page where a poem appears. When we are at an existential or psychological edge, the instability of subjectivity is potentially as dangerous as the chaos of a minor earthquake, and the rectangular shape of the page with its poem can be as reassuring as the doorframe in which we seek shelter.

The threshold is a place of transition; as such, it is a place of enormous vitality and activity as well as danger. Science provides its own analogue to thresholds—something biologists call the "margin effect," which notes that life energy concentrates and is more various at places of transition. Most marine life-forms inhabit the edges of the sea; more bird and animal species are found in that area where meadow blends with forest. Likewise, our nerves proliferate at the very edges of our bodies where skin meets world, and even more intimately, within our bodies, the greatest energy of chemical exchanges take place at the outer membrane of each body cell.

We also find the concept of the threshold in the social world. Recently a number of anthropologists, led by the late Victor Turner, have focused on the nature and role of liminal states in culture. "Liminal" means "threshold" and is applied to certain transitional states like marriages, funerals, and initiation ceremonies—states in which ordinary social rules are suspended and an individual may undergo profound changes in identity. Ritual processes guide individuals through this symbolic "space" of transformation, a space where social structures meet "anti-structure" much as, in poems, order meets disorder. The lyric poem follows these biological and anthropological models. At the threshold, linguistic, imaginative, and emotional energies are vastly heightened.

In our daily lives, the image of the threshold can be useful, too. The threshold is that place where we become aware that we are on the borderline between disorder and order. It can be like standing at the brink of a cliff, or the edge of an ocean, or the beginning of a love affair. In other words, it can be threat or thrill (or, perhaps most accurately, it is both at once).

On a day-to-day basis our threshold is constantly shifting and disappearing and being repressed out of anxiety, whereas in poetry we seek out poems that can take us to our threshold (or one of our thresholds). It is just such a place where we feel most alive, where both exchange of energy and change itself can happen. It is on a threshold, at the edge, where we are most able to alter our understanding of the world and of our own lives in it.

Readers and the Personal Threshold

The edge is what I have.

THEODORE ROETHKE, "In a Dark Time"

A lyric poet works to discover his or her threshold. She or he will write their best poems from there. Robert Frost urges poets to take the risk of discovering this authentic threshold when he says, "No tears in the writer, no tears in the reader. No surprise for the writer, no surprise for the reader" ("The Figure a Poem Makes"). He means if the poet isn't involved in a genuine way then the reader will not be either.

But what about the reader? Each individual reader has his or her own threshold. Like the poet's threshold, it is formed by two forces: one genetic, the other experiential. The genetic component has to do with our inborn temperament or personality and includes those attitudes and qualities that are biologically inherited. The experiential component concerns the way environment has affected or altered our basic temperament and has to do with events and experiences that have happened to us, especially during the formative years of childhood and adolescence.

The threshold is a different place for each reader, as it is for each poet. In commenting on the line "everything only connected by 'and' and 'and'" from Elizabeth Bishop's poem "Over 2,000 Illustrations and a Complete Concordance," the literary critic Denis Donoghue remarks:

> How much order or syntax a life needs is a personal matter: some lives get along quite well on the least degree of order compatible with its being order at all. Other lives have to have a pattern in place beforehand, so that every new experience fulfills a prior requirement. It would be possible to read Bishop's line in a tone of elation (as opposed to "random and pointless character of her experiences"), if you wanted your life to have a lot of risk and randomness. (*Connoisseurs of Chaos*, 271–72)

Some readers have a higher threshold for disorder and need more disordering in the poems they read. Others have a lower threshold and need a larger proportion of order to disorder in the poems that give them pleasure or that resonate meaningfully with their own experiences. The essential point is that for a poem to move us it must bring us near our own threshold. We must feel genuinely threatened or destabilized by the poem's vision of disordering, even as we are simultaneously reassured and convinced by its orderings.

Often arguments about taste, about whether a particular poem is "great" or not, simply have to do with differences in readers' thresholds. To say that we find a poet or a poem "boring" might be another way of saying it does not bring us close enough to any threshold. Or to say that a poem seems to us "meaningless chaos" might be another way of saying that it throws us way past our threshold.

Anxiety, Claustrophobia, and the Threshold

Imagine that we are back at our original image of pausing at the threshold of a house, a safe place to encounter and contemplate the power of disorder in our lives. But if I stroll too far out past my threshold, I may suddenly have a sense of being surrounded by disorder and feel that anxiety wild animals experience, the sense that danger exists in all 360 degrees of the world. It's what we see when a grazing deer suddenly lifts its head in a field: its bulged eyes roll back to see as much as they can; its ears rotate on tiny axes like radar antennae trying to perceive what could be approaching from behind where it cannot see.

By the same token, if we take half a dozen steps backward from the threshold into the middle of the room, we begin to feel claustrophobia. Our awareness of disorder diminishes to the overly safe; we are too secure. "Snug" becomes "smug," and the various and vivid world shrinks down to the rigid rectangle of the door shape— a chink of light and air, as though we squinted through the slit of an old armored headpiece.

Dancing on the Shore, Buffeting the Sea

Poets are drawn to and write from their thresholds, either inner or outer. In order to write well, a poet needs to go to that place where energy and intensity concentrate, that place just beyond which chaos and randomness reign.

The sea or ocean is perhaps the essential image from the outer world for disorder, and one of the best examples of a threshold in the natural world is a beach. Such a setting calls the spirit to play. You cannot help but see how free and excited children and even adults become on a summer beach: how much they enjoy being there at the edge where the solid order of sand meets the swirling chaos of breaking waves. To run in and out of the surf, to feel the force of the water's power or the foam swirling around your legs, to feel the sand sucked from under your feet so that you must dance to keep your balance—this is a vital delight known to most of us.

No one described this symbolic dimension of the seashore better than Walt Whitman, who grew up on rural Long Island and used to walk its beaches as boy and man:

Even as a boy, I had the fancy, the wish, to write a piece, perhaps a poem, about the sea-shore—that suggesting, dividing line, contact, junction, the solid marrying the liquid—that curious, lurking something, (as doubtless every objective form finally becomes to the subjective spirit) which means far more than its mere first sight, grand as that is—blending the real and ideal, and each made portion of the other. . . .

I must one day write a book expressing this liquid, mystic theme. Afterward, I recollect, how it came to me that instead of any special lyrical or epical or literary attempt, the seashore should be an invisible *influence*, a pervading gauge and tally for me, in my composition. ("Sea-Shore Fancies," in *Specimen Days*)

It may be that he never got to write the book that expressed "this liquid, mystic theme," but he certainly locates two of his greatest poems in this site of meeting and mingling. The climactic moment of his great poem on the theme of love, loss, poetry, and death,

"Out of the Cradle Endlessly Rocking," takes place on just such a beach in the moonlight. And his equally wonderful poem centered in the erotic mysteries, section 11 of "Song of Myself" ("Twenty-eight young men bathe by the shore . . ."), also locates itself at the seashore, where clothes and inhibitions can be shed and one can "dance" and "laugh" and embrace.

Whitman consciously intended that his readers go with him, not just to the beach threshold, but to venture further out than they were accustomed to going and thereby to stretch themselves and extend their spirits:

> Long have you timidly waded holding a plank by the shore,
> Now I will you to be a bold swimmer,
> To jump off in the midst of the sea, rise again, nod to me, shout, and
>   laughingly dash with your hair.
> ("Song of Myself," section 46)

Nor was Whitman alone in his commitment to push his threshold further out into the tumultuous sea. His great contemporary and fellow transformer of American poetry, Emily Dickinson, used the same imagery when she bid farewell to a childhood friend, not because they were separating physically, but because Emily sensed her own destiny involved far greater imaginative risks and joys than her cautious friend Abiah could handle:

> You are growing wiser than I am, and nipping in the bud fancies which I let blossom—perchance to bear no fruit, or if plucked, I may find bitter. The shore is safer, Abiah, but I love to buffet the sea—I can count the bitter wrecks here in these pleasant waters, and hear the murmuring winds, but oh, I love the danger! You are learning control and firmness. Christ Jesus will love you more. I'm afraid he don't love me *any*! (late 1850)

And with such ambivalent but brave feelings, Dickinson embarked on her bold adventure that yielded one of the greatest lyric treasures in our language.

It's probably safe to say that poets have a higher threshold for psychic disorder than the average population, just as professional dancers have higher pain thresholds than most of us. Not that I wish to minimize the perils of inner disorder. The novelist James Joyce once brought his schizophrenic daughter to the psychologist C. G. Jung. Jung, who was aware of Joyce's wildly experimental writing, which took great psychological risks, noted to the unhappy father: "Where you swim, she drowns." Nevertheless, it is precisely this higher tolerance that makes poets so useful to their culture. What they, pressing up against their thresholds, successfully assimilate into the formal and thematic orderings of poems, can, in turn, be absorbed by sympathetic readers.

CHAPTER FIVE

Bags Full of Havoc

In his poem "Journal for My Daughter," Stanley Kunitz describes his rambunctious friend—poet Theodore Roethke—as arriving "with his bags full of havoc." There's no better way to unpack these bags and see what varieties of chaos our poets have brought us than by quoting poems.

We could do worse than to begin by noting that most commentators since the dawn of history have felt that the great themes of the personal lyric are love and death. Once we move past the governing abstraction "love" into its multitudinous manifestations, it's as if we snorkeled above a tropical coral reef and saw below us the infinite variety of shapes and sizes and colors of fish.

We in the West have a long tradition of believing that romantic, passionate love can function as an ordering principle. We often experience our subjective lives as a quest for "true love," and feel that if we find someone we love and he or she loves us back, then our life and our world will cohere in a meaningful and exciting way. This quest is the theme of innumerable popular songs, movies, magazine articles, and books. This particular version of love as an ordering power derives mostly from a set of ideas and images "invented" by the troubadour poets of southern France around the end of the twelfth century. These poets wrote songs and poems about passionate, exclusive attachment to a single person; such devotion in "fin amor" was expected to make the (male) lover a better person, especially since the beloved was idealized and the lover-poet-knight sought to become worthy of her through noble deeds and courtly behavior. This troubadour concept of love spread quickly throughout Europe and gradually came to dominate Western thinking about romantic love, but even these idealized notions of harmonious mutual passion were shot through with more realistic information about erotic interaction between two people.

Think about jealousy as it echoes through the violent anguish and threat of Othello's musing about Desdemona: "And if you love me not, chaos is come again."

Or we might consider the ancient Greek opinion that passionate love was a form of mental illness. Aphrodite, the goddess of erotic love, was called "the unconquerable goddess" by the classical Greeks and was more feared for her power to disorder both social stabilities and individual lives than she was admired or worshipped.

Anyone who has been in love knows that there is as much misery and torment as joy involved. Even this small poem of William Blake's, which opens with an idealized description of selfless love, ends with a far more disquieting opinion of the same phenomenon:

The Clod & the Pebble

"Love seeketh not itself to please,
Nor for itself hath any care
But for another gives its ease,
And builds a heaven in hell's despair."

So sung a little clod of clay
Trodden with the cattle's feet
But a pebble of the brook
Warbled out these metres meet:

"Love seeketh only self to please
To bind another to its delight,
Joys in another's loss of ease
And builds a hell in heaven's despite."

And of course, love or desire is a complex phenomenon that lyric poets have often celebrated for its vitalizing power. Here's a Yaqui Indian love poem:

Many pretty flowers, red, blue, and yellow.
We say to the girls, "Let us go and walk among the flowers."

The wind comes and sways the flowers.
The girls are like that when they dance.
Some are wide-open, large flowers and some are tiny little flowers.
The birds love the sunshine and the starlight.
The flowers smell sweet.
The girls are sweeter than the flowers.
(from *The Sky Clears*, ed. A. Grove Day)

The above poem provides a good occasion to mention that simplicity and clarity of expression are often virtues in the personal lyric I am writing about. It's not that emotions aren't complex—they are. It's merely that part of the process of transforming one's emotions or experiences into a poem or song calls for a clarifying and simplifying that are themselves a major part of the ordering.

Here is a poem spoken by a woman and written down over three thousand years ago in the New Kingdom era in Egypt:

Love, how I'd love to slip down to the pond,
   bathe with you close by on the bank.
Just for you I'd wear my new Memphis swimsuit,
   made of sheer linen, fit for a queen—
Come see how it looks in the water!

Couldn't I coax you to wade in with me?
   Let the cool creep slowly around us?
Then I'd dive deep down
   and come up for you dripping,
Let you fill your eyes
   with the little red fish I'd catch.

And I'd say, standing there tall in the shallows:
   Look at my fish, love,
How it lies in my hand,
   How my fingers caress it,
slip down its sides . . .

But then I'd say softer,
   eyes bright with your seeing:
a gift, love. No words.

Come closer and
　　　　look, it's all me.
(trans. John L. Foster)

The following is an ancient Indian poem, originally written in San-skrit:

Traveller there's nothing
in this deaf village
but stones
you look out at the horizon clouds
and you see high
breasts
I can tell
if you feel like staying why don't you.
(from *The Peacock's Egg*, trans. W. S. Merwin and J. Moussaieff Masson)

A note to the above translation says: "The situation is that a traveller has asked a young woman for a place to pass the night. Her reply is punned: payodharonnati ("high looming clouds") also means 'high firm breasts.' She means that if her body appeals to him, he should spend the night with her, making love."

Japanese poetry is almost entirely lyric in nature. Its basic allegiance to the expression of subjectivity is apparent as early as the first imperial poetry anthology, the *Kokinshu*, compiled at the beginning of the tenth century. The anthologist, Ki no Tsurayuki (884–946), declares in his preface what he takes to be the most important characteristics of Japanese poetry:

The poetry of Japan has its roots in the human heart and flourishes in the countless leaves of words. Because human beings possess interests of so many kinds, it is in poetry that they give expression to the meditations of their hearts in terms of the sights appearing before their eyes and the sounds coming to their ears. Hearing the warbler sing among the blossoms and the frog in his fresh waters—is there any living being not given to song? It is poetry which, without exertion, moves heaven and earth, stirs the feelings of gods and spirits invisible to the eye, softens the relations between men and women, calms the hearts of fierce warriors. (Miner and Brower, *Japanese Court Poetry*)

A great number of the earliest poems in Japanese are love poems written by women. This fact, unfortunately, does not imply that the poetry of women was particularly valued in Japan. Early Japanese literary culture modeled itself on Chinese ideas and ideals, and thus Japanese males wrote their poems in Chinese, leaving the writing of the first poems in Japanese to aristocratic women. Thus, through an irony of cultural history, a denigrated language was first given poetic form by a demeaned sex. Here is a love poem written by the famous ninth-century woman poet Ono no Komachi:

> Although I come to you constantly
> over the road of dreams,
> those nights of love
> are not worth one waking touch of you.
> (trans. Kenneth Rexroth and Ikuko Atsumi)

The two-thousand-year-old Hebrew Song of Solomon is a poem structured as a dialogue between two lovers and begins with these words from the woman known as "the Shulamite":

> Kiss me, make me drunk with your kisses!
> Your sweet loving
> is better than wine.
>
> You are fragrant,
> you are myrrh and aloes.
> All the young women want you.
>
> Take me by the hand, let us run together!
> (trans. Ariel and Chana Bloch)

John Keats pleads the manipulative agony of desperate desire in these lines commonly entitled "Lines Supposed to Have Been Addressed to Fanny Brawne" (1819):

> This living hand, now warm and capable
> Of earnest grasping, would, if it were cold
> And in the icy silence of the tomb,
> So haunt thy days and chill thy dreaming nights

That thou wouldst wish thine own heart dry of blood
So in my veins red life might stream again,
And thou be conscience-calm'd—see, here it is—
I hold it towards you.

Or we have this whimsically anguished poem of love longing by
the twentieth-century Brazilian poet Carlos Drummond de An-
drade:

Don't Kill Yourself

Carlos, keep calm, love
is what you're seeing now:
today a kiss, tomorrow no kiss,
day after tomorrow's Sunday
and nobody knows what will happen
Monday.

It's useless to resist
or to commit suicide.
Don't kill yourself. Don't kill yourself!
Keep all of yourself for the nuptials
coming nobody knows when,
that is, if they ever come.

Love, Carlos, tellurian,
spent the night with you,
and now your insides are raising
an ineffable racket,
prayers,
victrolas,
saints crossing themselves,
ads for better soap,
a racket of which nobody
knows the why or wherefore.

In the meantime you go on your way
vertical, melancholy.
You're the palm tree, you're the cry
nobody heard in the theatre

and all the lights went out.
Love in the dark, no, love
in the daylight, is always sad,
sad, Carlos, my boy,
but tell it to nobody,
nobody knows nor shall know.
(trans. Elizabeth Bishop)

A potentially infinite list of poems about the various disordering powers of love might conclude with this couplet in which the ancient Roman poet Catullus records his intense ambivalence when in the grip of love:

I hate and I love. Maybe you ask how I can do it.
I don't know, but I feel it happen, and it's excruciating.
(trans. Peter Bing and Rip Cohen)

Death and Disorder

No more to walk the earth that feeds and eats us all.
HOMER, *The Iliad*

Along with love, death is seen as the other great traditional theme of lyric poetry. The German philosopher Hegel refers to death as "the most immediate and also the most comprehensive form of negation."

Religions often propose their grand ordering schemes in response to the disorder of death, and most cultures provide images of what happens to someone after he or she dies. Frequently, they are imagined to travel to the land of the dead. Such images are ordering and reassuring in the sense that they speak to what happens to the dead, but for the bereaved who are still alive, the emotions of grief and loss are extraordinarily painful and destabilizing. Alfred, Lord Tennyson's book-length lyric sequence *In Memoriam A. H. H.* was written as a means of coping with the death of his dearest friend, Arthur Hallam, who died at the age of twenty-three in 1832. Over the course of the next ten years, Tennyson wrote 131 brief lyrics that follow the progress of his grieving. Here is the seventh poem from the sequence, in which the poet visits the London house where his friend lived:

> Dark house, by which once more I stand
>   Here in the long unlovely street,
>   Doors, where my heart was used to beat
> So quickly, waiting for a hand,
>
> A hand that can be clasped no more—
>   Behold me, for I cannot sleep,
>   And like a guilty thing I creep
> At earliest morning to the door.
>
> He is not here; but far away
>   The noise of life begins again,
>   And ghastly through the drizzling rain
> On the bald street breaks the blank day.

Though Tennyson's sequence is instigated and propelled by intense thematic disorderings like grief and despair, each poem is structured with powerful *formal* orderings: each is written in four-line stanzas of iambic tetrameter with an *abba* rhyme scheme. This elaborate formal ordering is, in turn, partly rescued from sing-song tediousness by the disordering power of complicated syntax, the frequent pauses in midline, and the use of enjambment to make the end rhymes less obtrusive.

Or consider this haiku by the nineteenth-century Japanese poet Issa on the death of his daughter:

> The world of dew
> is the world of dew.
> And yet, and yet . . .

The world of dew is a Buddhist symbol for the material world. Since all earthly things must perish like the dew that vanishes each morning, Buddhism counsels emotional detachment as a defense against suffering. The first two lines of Issa's poem seem to accept the grim reality of the ephemeral, seem to say: what is true, is true. Even the form of Issa's "acceptance" in these lines has a mathematical "balance" to it: the world of dew equals the world of dew just as four equals four. But the final line pierces and bursts this bubble of apparent acquiescence with a heart-cry of grief that refuses to accept the terms of mortality without an anguished protest: "and yet, and yet . . ."

The following is a Bedouin song of grief from North Africa:

Under the earth of your grave you are hidden from sight,
    O Kheira
You are imprisoned in a house where there is only darkness
You have left Ahmed and his sister Mahjuba
You are gone, O beautiful one with earrings,
      gone not to come again
Your leg was like a lily
O woman like a gazelle.
(from *The Unwritten Song*, ed. Willard Trask)

The pre-Columbian Aztec civilization of Mexico placed great value on lyric poetry, regarding it as the highest art form. One convention of Aztec poetry involved uniting two words so frequently that they not only become synonyms but that they also evoke a third idea, usually a metaphor. Examples are "face-and-heart," which means personality, and "flower-and-song," which metaphorically means poetry, art, and symbolism. We see flower-and-song in the following poem in which the poet contemplates his own death and oblivion:

Will I have to go like the flowers that perish?
Will nothing remain of my name?
Nothing of my fame here on earth?
At least my flowers, at least my songs!
Earth is the region of the fleeting moment.
Is it also thus in the place
where in some way one lives [i.e., after death]?
Is there joy there, is there friendship?

Or is it only here on earth
we come to know our faces?
(from *Pre-Columbian Literatures of Mexico*, ed. Miguel León-Portilla)

In this Native American poem set by a river, the awareness that everything is mortal and perishes becomes the occasion for a moment of intimate and calm contemplation:

The earth is all that lives
And the earth shall not last.
We sit on a hillside, by the Greasy Grass
and our little shadow lies out in the blades
of grass, until sunset.

Certainly, if the thought of death can entail a fierce and terrifying disorder, then the condition of old age is also a disordering that imagination struggles against. The Irish poet William Butler Yeats felt passionately how bodily decrepitude called forth the power of song:

An aged man is but a paltry thing,
A tattered coat upon a stick, unless
Soul clap its hands and sing, and louder sing
For every tatter in its mortal dress . . .
("Sailing to Byzantium")

The following lament, from the Gond tribe of central India, has no such consolation:

How young I was
When I planted the mango
And the tamarind
And still their leaves are full of life
But there is none in my old body.
(from *The Unwritten Song*, ed. Trask)

Or this poem by the sixth-century B.C. Greek poet Anacreon:

I have gone gray at the temples,
yes, my head is white, there's nothing
of the grace of youth that's left me,
and my teeth are like an old man's.

Life is lovely. But the lifetime
that remains for me is little.
For this cause I mourn. The terrors
of the Dark Pit never leave me.
For the house of Death is deep down
underneath; the downward journey
to be feared, for once I go there
I know well there's no returning.

More Disorderings

Besides the traditional lyric themes of love and death, there are numerous other large subjects that introduce disturbing chaos into life and thus into poetry. Here is a poem by the contemporary Israeli poet Yehuda Amichai about the furiously disruptive power of war or terrorist violence:

The Diameter of the Bomb

The diameter of the bomb was thirty centimeters
and the diameter of its effective range about seven meters,
with four dead and eleven wounded.
And around these, in a larger circle
of pain and time, two hospitals are scattered
and one graveyard. But the young woman
who was buried in the city she came from,
at a distance of more than a hundred kilometers,
enlarges the circle considerably,
and the solitary man mourning her death
at the distant shores of a country far across the sea
includes the entire world in the circle.
And I won't even mention the howl of orphans

that reaches up to the throne of God and
beyond, making
a circle with no end and no God.
(trans. Chana Bloch and Stephen Mitchell)

Notice how Amichai's poem about the bomb works by repeatedly asserting the "perfect" geometry of the circle image, only to shatter its ordering power with the outward implications and consequences of human violence that finally overwhelm even the ultimate ordering principle of "God."

Emily Dickinson, one of the greatest poets of concentrated and extreme inner states, writes about the power of physical pain to abolish the orderly progression of objective time and institute a vast, subjective agony in its place:

Pain – expands the Time –
Ages coil within
The minute Circumference
Of a single Brain – (J. 967)

The poet Jane Kenyon, who died in 1995 at the age of forty-seven from leukemia, wrote movingly of the inner disorder of manic-depressive syndrome in a wonderful poem entitled "Having It Out with Melancholy." In another Kenyon poem, "Back," she writes about returning from depressive illness to the small and particular consolations of the world:

We try a new drug, a new combination
of drugs, and suddenly
I fall into my life again

like a vole picked up by a storm
then dropped three valleys
and two mountains away from home.

I can find my way back. I know
I will recognize the store
where I used to buy milk and gas.

I remember the house and barn,
the rake, the blue cups and plates,
the Russian novels I loved so much,

and the black silk nightgown
that he once thrust
into the toe of my Christmas stocking.

Here is a poem by the contemporary American poet Lisa Spaar
that takes on the subject of the self-starvation of anorexia nervosa:

Hallowe'en

On the night of skulled gourds,
of small, masked demons
begging at the door,
a man cradles his eldest daughter
in the family room. She's fourteen,
she's dying because she will not eat
anymore. The doorbell keeps ringing;
his wife gives the sweets away.
He rubs the scalp
through his girl's thin hair.
She sleeps. He does not know
what to do.
When the carved pumpkin
gutters in the windowglass,
his little son races through the room,
his black suit printed with bones
that glow in the dark.
His pillowsack bulges with candy,
and he yelps with joy.
The father wishes he were young.
He's afraid of the dream
she's burning back to,
his dream of her before her birth,
so pure, so perfect,
with no body to impede her light.

This poem by Molly Peacock dramatizes the previously taboo subjects of violence and alcoholism within families:

Valley of the Monsters

You might think I'm going to tell you where I've been,
but I'm writing about where I haven't been,

as yet. The Valley of the Monsters is a real place
where rocks are formed in monsters' shapes,

as clouds take the shapes people point to in the sky—
only the rocks, of course, are more permanent. To say why

I'm writing audaciously about what I haven't seen
will occupy the rest of ~~my life~~ this poem: the scene

is a kitchen where two dinosaurs, the kind with those little
lizardy hands and huge haunches, stand in the middle

of the floor guzzling beer and crushing the cans
with their scaly thumb-equivalents. Hah! I *can*

be audacious because I've been here before! I see
it's the Valley of the Monsters of my drunken family!

In fact, I grew up in the Valley of the Monsters, where
minds were formed in monsters' shapes, like what air

currents turn clouds into shapes in the sky people point at,
feeling lucky to have grasped the fragmentary, but

the minds of the monsters are far more permanent.
The rocks that form the real Valley of the Monsters are meant

to be paid for as a tourist attraction, whereas of course
my dinosaurs with beer cans are a matter of the coarse

substance of unpaid life. The curious thing about expression
is that simple telling of something begins the motion

of fulfilling the need to say it. Thus it is healthy
to speak, even in rhymes, about where we see

we're going, even if we haven't been there to find
our answers yet. The rocks are quite permanent, I find,

as is the need to expose them to the fantasy
of finding shapes in them, for fantasy is scrutiny.

In recent years, such poems as Allen Ginsberg's "Howl" have explored violence as an inextricable part of our culture. Even more recently, poets have begun to write personal lyrics about the suffering that emerges from racism, sexism, and gender issues. And there are also poems of simple sadness, which has the power to disorient our lives and undermine our sense of self. Here is one by the T'ang dynasty Chinese poet Po Chu-i:

Feelings Wakened by a Mirror

My beautiful one gave it to me when we parted,
but I leave the mirror stored in its box.
Since her flowering face left my sight,
autumn waters have no more lotus blooms.
For years I've never opened the box;
red dust coats the mirror's green bronze.
This morning I took it out and wiped it off,
peered into it at my haggard face,
and, done peering, went on to ponder sadly
the pair of twined dragons carved on its back.
(from *The Columbia Book of Chinese Poetry*)

The ninth-century Chinese poet Tu Mu writes this poem about the sadness of parting from a friend, a familiar theme of Chinese poetry:

Great love may seem like none at all:
wine before us, we only know that smiles won't come.
The tallow candle has a heart—it grieves at parting,
in our place drips tears until the break of day.

Delight in Disorder

Although we have just skimmed across a number of instances of destabilizing subject matter, it would be a great mistake to conclude that disorder is simply or primarily destructive. Often, it has the power to disrupt our lives in a vitalizing way, to jolt us out of ruts. Love poems especially celebrate the pleasurable chaos of erotic excitement, as in this seventeenth-century English poem by Robert Herrick:

Delight in Disorder

A sweet disorder in the dress
Kindles in clothes a wantonness.
A lawn about the shoulders thrown
Into a fine distraction;
An erring lace, which here and there
Enthralls the crimson stomacher;
A cuff neglectful, and thereby
Ribbons to flow confusedly;
A winning wave, deserving note,
In the tempestuous petticoat;
A careless shoestring, in whose tie
I see a wild civility;
Do more bewitch me than when art
Is too precise in every part.

Among the other affirmative forms of disordering that poems embody, we could number this odd poem by Wallace Stevens (1879–1955), which is a hymn in praise of imagination's vital eccentricity:

Disillusionment of Ten O'Clock

The houses are haunted
By white night-gowns.
None are green,
Or purple with green rings,
Or green with yellow rings,
Or yellow with blue rings.

None of them are strange,
With socks of lace
And beaded ceintures.
People are not going
To dream of baboons and periwinkles.
Only, here and there, an old sailor,
Drunk and asleep in his boots,
Catches tigers
In red weather.

Or this poem by the Chilean poet Pablo Neruda, which simultaneously celebrates a humble object in the world and enacts the joys of imagination through its delirious flurry of metaphors:

Ode to My Socks

Maru Mori brought me
a pair
of socks
which she knitted herself
with her sheep-herder's hands,
two socks as soft
as rabbits.
I slipped my feet
into them
as though into
two
cases
knitted
with threads of
twilight
and goatskin.
Violent socks,
my feet were
two fish made
of wool,
two long sharks
seablue, shot
through

by one golden thread,
two immense blackbirds,
two cannons,
my feet
were honored
in this way
by
these
heavenly
socks.
They were
so handsome
for the first time
my feet seemed to me
unacceptable
like two decrepit
firemen, firemen
unworthy
of that woven
fire,
of those glowing
socks.

Nevertheless
I resisted
the sharp temptation
to save them somewhere
as schoolboys
keep
fireflies,
as learned men
collect
sacred texts,
I resisted
the mad impulse
to put them
in a golden
cage

and each day give them
birdseed
and pieces of pink melon.
Like explorers
in the jungle who hand
over the very rare
green deer
to the spit
and eat it
with remorse,
I stretched out
my feet
and pulled on
the magnificent
socks
and then my shoes.

The moral
of my ode is this:
beauty is twice
beauty
and what is good is doubly
good
when it is a matter of two socks
made of wool
in winter.
(trans. Robert Bly)

Awe, Risk, and Joy

Knud Rasmussen, the Danish explorer, gathered the following poems among the Eskimo and Inuit and included them in his 1930 report on his expedition. He noted that the composing of poems was extremely important to these people: "Every man and woman, sometimes even children, had his own poems: and this despite the fact that it is justifiably regarded as a large-scale and difficult task to create a good new song."

Constantly facing fierce living conditions and the frequent prospect of starvation, they were often impelled toward risk-taking to
save their lives:

Hunger

Fear hung over me.
I dared not try
to hold out in my hut.

Hungry and chilled,
I stumbled inland,
tripping, falling constantly.

At Little Musk Ox Lake
the trout made fun of me;
they wouldn't bite.

On I crawled,
and reached the Young Man's River
where I caught salmon once.

I prayed
for fish or reindeer
swimming in the lake.

My thoughts
reeled into nothingness,
like run-out fishing-line.

Would I ever find firm ground?
I staggered on,
muttering spells as I went.
(Kingmerut, a Copper Eskimo man, Ellis River)

Polar Bear

I saw a polar bear
on an ice-drift.
He seemed harmless as a dog,
who comes running toward you,

wagging his tail.
But so much
did he want to get at me
that when I jumped aside
he went spinning on the ice.
We played this game of tag
from morning until dusk.
But then, at last, I tired him out,
and ran my spear into his side.
(Aua, an Iglulik Eskimo man, Lyon Inlet)

These same people felt and celebrated a natural beauty whose vast scale threatened to overwhelm them with an emotion we might call awe:

Song

And I thought over again
My small adventures
As with a shore-wind I drifted out
In my kayak
And thought I was in danger.

My fears,
Those small ones
That I thought so big
For all the vital things
I had to get and to reach.

And yet, there is only
One great thing,
The only thing:
To live to see in huts and on journeys
The great day that dawns
And the light that fills the world.
(from *The Unwritten Song*, ed. Trask)

We could do worse than to close this small anthology of disturbing and vitalizing disorders with an eighth-century Chinese poem celebrating the pleasures of gentle drunkenness:

Written When Drunk

Once drunk, my delight knows no limits,
so much better than before I'm drunk.
My movements all are shaped like dances,
and everything I say comes out a poem!
(Chang Yueh, 667–730)

The Shell of Song

In book 5 of his long autobiographical poem *The Prelude*, Wordsworth described a dream in which he was wandering alone in a desert:

> I saw before me stretched a boundless plain
> Of sandy wilderness, all black and void,
> And as I looked around, distress and fear
> Came creeping over me, when at my side,
> Close at my side, an uncouth shape appeared
> Upon a dromedary, mounted high.
> He seemed an Arab of the Bedouin tribes:
> A lance he bore, and underneath one arm
> A stone, and in the opposite hand a shell
> Of a surpassing brightness. (ll. 71–79)

Participating fully in the magical logic of his dream, the poet understands that these two objects, the stone and the shell, are "books" the Arab is going to take to a safe place to bury, because a great flood is coming. And what are these books?

> . . . the Arab told me that the stone
> Was "Euclid's Elements"; and "This," said he,
> "Is something of more worth"; and at the word
> Stretched forth the shell, so beautiful in shape,
> In colour so resplendent, with command
> That I should hold it to my ear. I did so,
> And heard that instant in an unknown tongue,

Which yet I understood, articulate sounds,
A loud prophetic blast of harmony;
An Ode, in passion uttered, which foretold
Destruction to the children of the earth
By deluge, now at hand. (ll. 86–98)

The stone is geometry; the shell, poetry. Yes, we think, in the metaphorical world of dream symbols, Euclid's geometry might well be a rock—a self-contained system, unitary, solid, absolute. All that mathematics had accomplished and all that humankind still hoped for from its ally, science. An order that transcended the limits of this world and "wedded soul to soul in purest bond / Of reason, undisturbed by space or time" (ll. 104–5). But the shell? Lift the shell to your ear and you hear what? The ocean; its quiet roar. (Never mind, of course, that this is the echo of your own ear you hear.) The Arab informs the dreamer that poetry has the power to prophesy the future—the flood he is listening to *inside* the shell is *even now* in the outer world slipping apocalyptically across the dunes toward them and can be seen glittering in the far distance. Poetry, with its prophetic power, must also be saved so that civilization can continue.

When we lift Wordsworth's shell to our ear, we hear destructive energy contained within the graceful convolutions of artistic form. The flood that might have overwhelmed us (was it subjective passion or objective deluge?) has itself been transformed from vast, watery apocalypse into rhythmic sound contained within a powerful shape. The shell that was tossed about in the real ocean has now become an object capable of taking the ocean inside it and taming it. No, not entirely taming it: the flood is still real, still sliding across the sands toward the two figures, who now begin to flee together. Mathematics, with its absolute, transcendent orderings is one model for understanding the world—it "explains" the smooth movements of the stars and planets. But its order is absolute, nonhuman. Poetry, which is capable of incorporating inner disorder ("passion") and outer disorder (the deluge) within its forms, is a model that "explains" a human and earthbound universe—one that conforms to our limit-conditions of time, space, bodies. The dreamer's task is to save Euclid and poetry, the stone and the shell. But only the shell also has the power to save the dreamer.

CHAPTER SIX

The Two Survivals

> I don't believe that poetry can save the world. I do believe
> that the forces in us wish to share something of our
> experience by turning it into something and giving it to
> somebody: that is poetry. That is some kind of saving
> thing, and as far as my life is concerned, poetry has saved
> meq again and again.
>
> MURIEL RUKEYSER

Risk is involved when a lyric poet feels and expresses
emotion or writes about a disturbing experience. An instability ac-
companies the project. But instability is built into the inner workings
of our consciousness, and it is omnipresent in the external world also.

The difference between a lyric poet and a person who does not
write poems is that the poet has an arena in which to focus his
or her encounter with disorder. And the poet's struggle to engage
disorder with the ordering powers of imagination and the cultural
tool of language leads to a sense of having mastered subjectivity and
restabilized the self.

What's more, *every* encounter with disorder of any sort that results
in a poem is a successful encounter in the most basic sense we can
mean it—namely, the poet survived. The very fact of the poem's
existence on the page is proof of its efficacy for survival, proof that the
poet succeeded in ordering his or her disorder (if only briefly); proof
a person could take on the thematic disorder of that particular poem
(even the theme of madness) and order it. If the poet had failed or
perished in the attempt, we would not be reading his or her poem.
It's that simple and that strangely lovely.

Of course, someone rushes forward and says, "Fine, but a month later the poet committed suicide." So what? We don't say planes can't fly because planes occasionally crash. People commit suicide with sad frequency, but such an act is not correlated with their being poets. Quite the contrary, all the testimony from poets is that the ordering powers of lyric poetry have given them precious resources to encounter the jeopardies and disorders that assail all humans.

Connecting

> The plucked chord performs its natural duty: it sounds!
> It calls for an echo from one that feels alike.
> J. G. VON HERDER, "Essay on the Origin of Language"

> The voice of the solitary
> Who makes others less alone.
> STANLEY KUNITZ, "Revolving Meditation"

The lyric poem's primary victory is scored for the poet him- or herself. Writing the poem helped her to survive, helped him to live. This initial personal triumph is followed by the extension of the poem into the larger social world of readers and audience, where the second survival power is made manifest.

Readers are only "saved" by poems that enter deeply into them, and this happens when sympathetic identification of reader with writer takes place. The history of the idea of sympathy is central to the rise of the personal lyric in the West in the eighteenth century, but it's too vast and complex to elaborate here. Still, we should note that Adam Smith, in his *Theory of Moral Sentiments* (1759), sees sympathy as the bridge of imagination that connects up separate embodied selves and thus is the basis of all morality. And Rousseau announces, "How are we moved to pity? By getting outside our-selves and identifying with a being who suffers"; and, "He who imagines nothing is aware only of himself; he is isolated in the midst of mankind" ("Essay on the Origin of Language," 1755). This imag-inative ability to identify ourselves with other people is not only the moral touchstone of humanism but also the psychological mechanism underlying all lyric efficacy. Few grasped this fact as deeply as Whitman, who opens his great lyric sequence "Song of Myself" with a basic solicitation of the reader's sympathetic identification:

> I celebrate myself, and sing myself,
> And what I assume you shall assume,
> For every atom belonging to me as good belongs to you.

"Become me," urges Whitman, become the "I" of this poem for this poem's duration. Only then will its wonders and powers be revealed to you and become a part of you.

And William Carlos Williams, at the beginning of his book *Spring and All* (1923), negotiates directly and intimately with his readers about what will happen next: "In the imagination, we are from henceforth (so long as you read) locked in a fraternal embrace, the classic caress of author and reader. We are one. Whenever I say 'I' I mean also 'you.' And so, together, as one, we shall begin" (178).

WHEN I MOMENTARILY yield my sense of separateness and become the "I" of a lyric poem, I share the poet's feelings and thoughts, am buffeted by the same disorderings. Likewise, I am sustained and consoled by the knowledge that we have survived: have come through, lucid and alive, to the poem's conclusion.

But we can be even more specific about the nature of the victory we share with the poem. When the poem succeeds in incorporating disorder without disintegrating into chaos or silence, I, the reader, am given both courage and hope. It is possible that such terms as "courage" and "hope" seem disturbingly naive for something as supposedly sophisticated as the reading of poems, but I would suggest that, on the contrary, these qualities are essential if we wish to live fully. To be *encouraged*, in the deep sense of being inspired with courage and confidence, is a profound spiritual and emotional experience.

I'm talking now not about "great" poems; that is, poems we are told to admire by teachers and authorities. Instead, I mean poems that we personally love deeply. The poems that matter enormously to us and that help us live. Through these poems, we recognize ourselves in an "other." Through these poems, we are brought to thresholds inside us we might never approach without their help.

We need only think of specific examples where a kinship between poet and reader might be operative. If I am afflicted with manic-depressive disorder, a poem of Jane Kenyon's like "Having It Out with Melancholy" or "Back" can tell me I am not alone in my situation. Her poems present not just the evidence of her survival but a dramatization of the very act of engaging her misery and confusion and responding to it with dignity and shaping imagination. If I were struggling with anorexia, Lisa Russ-Spaar's "Hallowe'en" or Louise Glück's "Dedication to Hunger" could be crucial to my ability to survive, not in the manner of health professionals or self-help books even, but because I am hearing another version of my experience spoken by an authentic voice *within* that experience.

Only lyric poetry is equal to the perverse complexities of human psychology that can lead to such strange insights as this one drama-tized by Emily Dickinson, where a "positive" emotion like joy is far more destabilizing than grief:

> I can wade Grief—
> Whole Pools of it—
> I'm used to that—
> But the least push of Joy
> Breaks up my feet— (J. 252)

Dickinson may truthfully claim that "the least push of Joy" destroys her emotional equilibrium in the world of experience, but in the world of patterned language where poetry helps her survive, she is nimble and alert.

IT SHOULDN'T BE thought that either the poet's survival or the lis-tener's must necessarily be taking place at the precise moment a crisis is occurring. Often a poet cannot deal with certain disorder-ings until a good while after they have taken place. Such a project of delayed encounter may well be behind Wordsworth's famous definition of poetry as "emotion recollected in tranquillity." His formulation imagines the poet circling back from the safe place of "tranquillity" to again engage the volatile emotions that so destabilized him long ago. In such a project of engaging long-vanished but significant disturbances, poetry is especially useful because language has the power to conjure lost ones out of the air and make the absent become present again.

Silence and Suffering

> My sickness is when words draw in their horns and the physical world refuses to be ordered, recreated, arranged and selected. I am a victim of it then, not a master.
> SYLVIA PLATH

Speech is among the most fundamental ways we have of connecting our selves to other selves. There are silences that are positive and powerful and willed by the self, but many silences have a destructive origin and destructive consequences. They are the result of shame, or fear, or inhibition. In the silence of shame, we imagine that if others knew our story they would recoil in disgust or disapproval. Or we can be inhibited by the sense that our experiences have no significance or value. In the silence of fear, it is possible to feel that we are still in danger from hurtful people in our past, or that speaking of something will cause hurt to people we care about. There is also the silence of oblivion: a sense that cherished people and things have vanished and we are powerless to recover them.

Often these silences are connected to a sense that survival depends on them. That we will be stronger by being silent. Or that being silent is the only way we can survive. We think that, in order to successfully endure our suffering, we must not speak, even to ourselves. And yet, this silence makes us the victim of our experience, not the master. We cannot master experience until we acknowledge its true nature and dimensions: both the facts of what happened and the emotions associated with those facts.

To suffer in silence, like grieving in silence, is destructive of the self, since it means walling off aspects of experience and the emotions connected with them. No one and nothing can prevent suffering, loss, and confusion in life. These phenomena are simply a part of human experience. It is the destructive or isolating silence that arrives in the aftermath of such experiences that can be changed.

Secrets and Poetry

Poetry is where we meet to share our secrets.
STANLEY KUNITZ

When we, as individuals, have secrets, they are often painful or awkward memories—in other words, stories saturated with shame or embarrassment. Such secrets, kept from others, have the power to isolate us, to lock us up in alienation. When we bond deeply with another person, become his or her best friend, one of the rituals that symbolizes the mutual trust of such a relationship is the reciprocal sharing of secrets. Each person is vulnerable in that moment of sharing, and the mutual risk involved in this exchange is extraordinary. When my best friend carries my secrets, he or she has a part of me in trust, and vice versa. But also, once I have shared my secret, my sense of isolation and separateness has been subtly but deeply altered—I am no longer isolated. By sharing my secret, and having it accepted without judgment or rebuff—in fact, having it accepted with sympathy—I can take a small step from survival toward healing; a step analogous to the one a poet makes when he or she first shares poems with another reader or an audience.

Conversely, when we hoard our secrets, we intensify our sense of separateness and isolation from others. We can even keep secrets from ourselves, and this can have survival consequences. On April 18, 1999, the *New York Times* reported on a study of patients who suffered midlife panic and hypertension attacks. The study examined a treatment that involved talk therapy in which the patients discovered painful, suppressed memories from childhood. Often the patients were unaware of the memories when treatment began but remembered them as they talked with therapists—which is to say, the patients had kept secrets from themselves. According to this study, the talk therapy leading to the discovery and expression of these memories was as effective or more so than treatment with antidepressants.

Disclosure and Healing

Jesus said, "If you bring forth what is within you, what you bring forth will save you. If you do not bring forth what is within you, what you do not bring forth will destroy you."
The Gnostic Gospel of Thomas

For the past decade or more, the American social psychologist James W. Pennebaker has been investigating the connections between "disclosure" and physical as well as emotional health: "In the psychological and medical literatures, there is overwhelming evidence that traumatic experiences provoke mental and physical health problems. A central tenet of most psychotherapies is that talking about these experiences is beneficial" (*Emotion, Disclosure and Health*, 3). He goes on to say that physical and emotional improvement takes place regardless of the kind of therapy the patient is undergoing, probably because the very act of translating experience into language is empowering to the patient: "An important nonspecific feature of therapy is that it allows individuals to translate their experiences into words. The disclosure process itself, then, may be as important as any feedback the client receives from the therapist." Although conclusive scientific experiments in this area are difficult to design and control, there is mounting evidence that disclosure of painful or traumatic experience, in writing or speech, has a stimulating effect on the body's immune system.

We are only beginning to understand the ways in which speech and writing are connected to the physical well-being of our embodied selves. An article in the April 1999 issue of the *Journal of the American Medical Association* examined the effect of writing on people with chronic illnesses. Two groups of people were studied: one group suffering from rheumatoid arthritis and the second from asthma. Each illness group was further divided into two separate groups, the first of which (group one) was instructed to write for twenty minutes on three consecutive days on the topic, "the most painful incident in my life." Group two was instructed to write for twenty minutes on three consecutive days on the topic, "what I plan to do today." Before the writing assignment, all the participants were given careful medical examinations by doctors who knew nothing about the study and its purposes. Four months *after* the writing exercise, the participants were again examined by the doctors and their medical conditions compared with their earlier state. A total of 140 patients were involved. Members of group one, who wrote about the most painful incident in their lives, showed the following results in their subsequent medical exams:

47.1 percent showed significant improvement
48.6 percent showed no change
 4.3 percent were worse than before

Group two, the control group that wrote about its plans for the day, showed the following:

24.3 percent showed significant improvement
54.1 percent showed no change
21.6 percent were worse than before

Not only did group one show a startling 23 percent difference in the category of "significant improvement," but to that should be added the 17 percent who might, in the ordinary course of that time, have been expected to get worse but instead showed no decline.

Group one's assigned topic was not specific beyond the term "most painful incident in my life." Interestingly, none of the group chose to write about his or her illness. Instead, they chose as any collection of humans so instructed might have: they wrote about deaths of loved ones, intimate losses and hurts, and the agonies of unrequited love. In short, they gave expression to focused moments of anguish, to whatever existential crisis in their life approached closest to trauma, and this act of expression and storytelling improved their physical health.

The Spectrum of Disclosure

The studies cited above document the ability of disclosure to mobilize healing powers by allowing individuals to speak or write about painful, taboo subjects. Building on these studies, we could construct a spectrum of autobiographical disclosure to highlight the special role of poetry as an important way of responding to suffering and trauma.

At the extreme left of our spectrum, we have the alienated, shamed, or fearful silence of the victim who feels powerless to overcome his or her silence. At the extreme right, we have poetry (specifically, the personal lyric), which is the most highly patterned and complexly organized use of language known to humans:

silence ——>	*speech* ——>	*writing* ————————————>		
silence	blurted	diary	shaped narrative	poetry
(shame, fear,	disclosure	journal	or memoir	
or guilt)				

Beginning at the far left, in the depths of silence, we move to the right and arrive at our first overt disclosure, which I'll call "blurted speech." Blurted speech as a way of speaking about one's traumatic experience might take place in a bar or a therapeutic situation, or any number of other circumstances when opportunity appears or impulse insists. Such a spoken disclosure, like most spontaneous speech, is loosely organized and depends as much on gesture and tone of voice as it does on precise words to communicate its message.

As we move further to the right, we arrive at written language. Perhaps the most informal or least organized disclosure writing would take place in a diary or journal. As we go further to the right, we might see disclosure in the more organized written form of memoir, where the narrative is shaped and ordered according to principles of effective dramatic writing and words are chosen more carefully.

As we arrive at the far end of our spectrum, the autobiographical material of the personal lyric has undergone the extreme and complex linguistic and imaginative patterning that is the hallmark of all poetries. This patterning necessitates, among other things, careful attention to accurate and economical word choice, to the expressive possibilities of rhythm, to the dramatic unfolding of story, and to the descriptive vividness and symbolic power of details.

The spectrum of disclosure I've sketched above is no more than a commonsense progression. You might think that people would proceed gradually, incrementally through the various stages of linguistic organization as they struggled to express what haunts them, but what's really interesting is that so many people go *directly* from the extreme of traumatic or painful silence to the opposite extreme, poetry. It's as if, by instinctively choosing poetry, they are validating Emily Dickinson's observation: "After great pain, a formal feeling comes."

Perhaps the elaborate and intense patterns of poetry can also make people feel safe. Related to this, it's possible to say that the enormous disordering power of trauma needs or demands an equally powerful ordering to contain it, and poetry offers such order.

CHAPTER SEVEN

The Powers of Poetry

Each culture has its own preferences or rules as to what constitutes the formal orderings of a lyric. For much of the sixteenth through the nineteenth centuries, poetry in English was felt to be most properly constituted by accentual syllabic meter and rhyme. On the other hand, Chinese lyric poetry of the T'ang dynasty (700–950 A.D.) was defined by a whole different set of formal concepts. It not only had to have a set number of characters per line and a set number of lines (eight), but also had to exhibit an elaborate syntactical patterning: the four lines in the middle needed to form couplets that were syntactically parallel and at the same time conceptually and tonally contrasting or even antithetical. This Tu Fu poem from the eighth century illustrates these principles:

A Traveler at Night Writes His Thoughts

Delicate grasses, faint wind on the bank;
stark mast, a lone night boat:
stars hang down, over broad fields sweeping;
the moon boils up, on the great river flowing.
Fame—how can my writings win me that?
Office—age and sickness have brought it to an end.
Fluttering, fluttering—where is my likeness?
Sky and earth and one sandy gull.

Hebrew poetry of the Psalms likewise relies on the formal principle of several sorts of syntactical parallelism rather than on rhyme or meter:

Lift up your heads, O gates!
>   and be lifted up, O ancient doors!
>   that the King of glory may come in.
Who is the King of glory?
>   The LORD, strong and mighty,
>   the LORD, mighty in battle!
Lift up your heads, O gates!
>   and be lifted up, O ancient doors!
>   that the King of glory may come in.

(Psalm 24, Revised Standard Version)

Such culture-specific preferences are very important, of course. They give a culture's poetry its unique textures. But beneath these idiosyncratic principles there are three abiding and primordial powers that shape language into poems regardless of the culture: story, symbol, and incantation. These three powers are ancient, yet, like the personal lyric itself, they have persisted for millennia and underlie almost all personal lyrics.

It may be that the production of stories and symbols is innate to the way the human brain functions in the course of making meanings. And the omnipresence of incantation may well derive from an underlying, physiological dimension of soothing through rhythmic repetition.

Saying the Unsayable: The Power of Story

> Men reveal themselves in deeds and acts.
> ARISTOTLE, *Poetics*

If someone asked us, "What was your summer like?" we might answer: boring, exciting, interesting. These characterizations of our experience are labels. If the person inquired further, we would probably tell them a story: a selected narrative of events that took place, deeds we did. We might weave in weather and geography, disasters or delights, high and low points. We would also give our story focus—*we* ourselves would probably be the focus (after all, the acquaintance asked what *our* summer had been like). It wouldn't be the complete narrative, but a selection and arrangement designed to clarify its overall significance for us (what we had earlier called "boring" or "interesting" or "exciting"). When we try to communicate the meaning and significance of our experience (to others or to ourselves), we are likely to tell a story. Story is the most primordial way of establishing the meaning of what it is to be a self in a world of time, space, and other selves. Here is the anthropologist Clifford Geertz writing on and quoting the psychologist and educational theorist Jerome Bruner:

> Telling stories, about ourselves and about others, to ourselves and to others, is "the most natural and the earliest way in which we organize our experience and our knowledge" (Bruner). . . .
>
> The heart of the matter, what the learner learns whatever the teacher teaches, is that "human beings make sense of the world by telling stories about it—by using the narrative mode for construing reality. . . ." Tales are tools, "instruments of mind on behalf of meaning making. . . ."
>
> Our immediate experience, what happened yesterday or the day before, is framed in the same storied way. Even more striking, we represent our lives (to ourselves as well as to others) in the form of narrative. (*New York Review of Books*, April 10, 1997)

Story is not simply a narrative of chronological events. Story selects and arranges (or rearranges) details and events and gestures for their symbolic significance. In prose narrative, "more is more" because the goal is often to establish the complex richness and variety of the world of experience. In lyric story, "less is more." Everything that does not add to the intended dramatization is stripped away, and meaning is compressed into action and detail that reveal significance. Only that part of the world that heightens the dramatic focus is kept. Thus Aristotle in his *Poetics* says that if some part of a poem is removed and someone reading the poem doesn't notice a gap or absence, then that part was never a genuine part of the poem after all.

Aristotle also locates the heart of story in conflict. In lyric poetry, such conflict needn't be anything melodramatic. Merely introducing two pronouns into the opening line of a poem creates the tension essential to story: "I saw you in the diner . . ." There is a subtle, unresolved tension between the "I" and the "you" that seeks to be developed and resolved. You can see how subtle but real that tension is if you substitute a unitary pronoun: "We went to the diner." The reader may still be curious about what will happen next, may even be curious about who the "we" is, but the story tension created by the I/you has disappeared. It is this tension or conflict that is at the heart of story, providing story with dramatic focus.

Unlike narrative, which can have numerous characters, story in the personal lyric will have only two or three characters in order to establish and maintain dramatic focus and thereby communicate the story of the self. Here's a personal lyric by Theodore Roethke that structures itself around story:

My Papa's Waltz

The whiskey on your breath
Could make a small boy dizzy;
But I hung on like death:
Such waltzing was not easy.

We romped until the pans
Slid from the kitchen shelf;
My mother's countenance
Could not unfrown itself.

The hand that held my wrist
Was battered on one knuckle;
At every step you missed
My right ear scraped a buckle.

You beat time on my head
With a palm caked hard by dirt,
Then waltzed me off to bed
Still clinging to your shirt.

Notice how the dramatic facts of whiskey and whirling create the child's dizziness and disorientation. By stanza three, there are verbs that hint at violence: "battered," which of course refers to the father's knuckles, but what caused that battering we don't know. And "battered" is linked by alliteration to "buckle" two lines later, where the quiet violence of the scraped ear begins to subtly connect a violence against the child to the father's action (his missteps cause the boy's injuries). And then, in the final stanza, "beating" takes place, though this is all in "good fun." Now, have I exaggerated ridiculously the disorder of violence in this story of a scene in the family kitchen? Have I made a mountain out of a molehill? Yes and no. Of course, the poem is also celebratory of the father's clowning exuberance. But over the years, I have come to find that my students "read" the details and gestures of this story according to their own experiences in childhood. Those who have grown up in a family where alcohol was present in a consistently or sporadically disruptive way are invariably sensitive to the implications of the violence the boy experiences and of his relative powerlessness in relation to his father's size and actions. For them, it's not simply rambunctious-ness on the father's part, but something a bit more scary. And the mother's disapproval isn't just momentary and under her control, but is a deeply-dug-in response to the father's behavior (she *could not* "unfrown" herself) that has its own destructive implications for the boy. Nor is the conflict and tension resolved by any action that reconciles the key figures of father, mother, and child. Whether or not the child's awe is tinged with terror, it's easy to see that the poem's story enables Roethke to dramatize a complicated family dynamic and in the process to restabilize a self made "dizzy" by the experience.

I say that the conflict between characters is not resolved by any reconciling action, but it is important to note that the formal order-ing of meter and rhyme interacts with the disorder of the poem's actions and details. Likewise, there is the image of the waltz it-self. Dance is, by its very nature, patterned movement, and the waltz is surely among the most stately and "ordered" of Western dances.

Roethke's remembered dance dramatizes a self caught up in the shaping forces of childhood events. In this poem by Thomas Hardy, the poet is again a child, again is dancing in a long-ago time. But here we are clearly looking at another motive for stories: rescuing a cherished moment from the oblivion of the Vanished Past.

The Self Unseeing

Here is the ancient floor,
Footworn and hollowed and thin,
Here was the former door
Where the dead feet walked in.

She sat here in her chair,
Smiling into the fire;
He who played stood there,
Bowing it higher and higher.

Childlike, I danced in a dream;
Blessings emblazoned that day;
Everything glowed with a gleam;
Yet we were looking away!

The scene is celebrated even as it opens itself to a heartbreaking sense of inevitable and irreparable loss.

When I speak about story in lyric I don't mean simply narrative, but narrative crystallized and constellated around a lyric center. In the sense that I am using the word, narrative in poetry is a journey: each sentence pushes the discovery further in order to find something new. It is like the old song we used to sing when I was a kid: "The bear went over the mountain, to see what he could see. . . ." The motive is to push further and disclose new information or action. What happens next, what happens next, the narrative asks? Even though the language in a lyric moves down the page in time like a narrative, it is also constellating or crystallizing around an implicit or explicit center: an image, a scene, a thing or event. Story in a lyric poem has a centripetal impulse. It wishes to disclose meaning by focusing on something central and leaving out peripheral details unless they reinforce the central subject. Thus the Hardy poem quoted above centers around the scene by the firelight, and the Roethke poem around the kitchen scene and the image of waltzing. This distinction between narrative and what I am calling story is easier to intuit than to explain; it can best be sensed by asking if there is a single scene, image, or object around which the poem's conflict seems to be centered.

Story in lyric begins to assert its ordering powers in its opening lines and title, which usually make use of the physical ordering powers of orientation, information, and location. Roethke's title, "My Papa's Waltz," gives a great deal of information at the outset— it tells us that the focus is autobiographical ("My"), that the father is a central figure, and that a patterned dance will be a further focus of the poem. The ordering orientation and information in this title is immediately modified and disrupted by the opening line's reference to drunkenness: "The whiskey on your breath."

One of the pleasures of story is that the reader inhabits the poem's sensory setting: feels, sees, hears, tastes what the poem experiences. The great Spanish poet Federico García Lorca tells us the poet must be "a professor of the senses," punning on the poet's need to be both knowledgeable and enthusiastic about sensory details and specifics. This use of physical language to communicate meaning in story is in major contrast to how philosophy makes meanings out of language. One way philosophy orders the rich variety and chaos of experience is by using abstract language to cover over a vast and various territory of experience with a single word. There are thousands of different kinds of flowers: peonies, roses, tulips, daisies, dandelions, and so on. "Rose" is a specific noun and directs our attention to a specific flower in the world. But we could include roses, daisies, and tulips in a single term if we move from specific nouns to general nouns and use the word "flower." We thus achieve a kind of ordering by generalizing, but we are still connected to the physical world through the shared qualities of flowers (petal, stamen, etc.). If we take one further linguistic step, and it is a step philosophy often urges us to take, we will leave the physical world entirely and enter the world of abstract language. Thus we might go from "flowers" to "beauty."

Beauty is an idea. Perhaps it is an important idea, but for all its apparent grandeur, the term "beauty" has no connection to the physical world. Philosophy can construct whole fabrics of interrelated abstractions and generalized statements in its quest for its own sorts of ordering. Story, on the other hand, goes in the opposite direction in its search for meanings. Beauty in story is always a matter of embodiment and "sensuous incarnation" in details and specifics: of who, what, where, and when. Ezra Pound, advising young poets in the early years of the twentieth century, urged them to seek the "luminous detail" and to "go in fear of abstractions." A hundred years before Pound, William Blake gave this commitment to the physical world an ethical dimension:

> Labour well the Minute Particulars: attend to the Little Ones. . . .
> He would do good to another must do it in Minute Particulars.
> General Good is the plea of the scoundrel, hypocrite & flatterer,
> For Art & Science cannot exist but in minutely organized Particulars.
> ("Jerusalem")

Story is both a primal, concrete way of ordering experience and also a way of opening the self to disorder. When lyric ceases to hide behind abstraction (like Blake's scoundrels) and descends down into the chaos and specifics of the physical world to seek its meanings, it is another way that it has of making itself vulnerable to disorder.

ONE OF STORY'S primary purposes is to lay claim to experience. Autobiographical storytelling can take personal experience back from silence, shame, fear, or oblivion. It says, "I cherish this," or, "This haunts me." It asserts the significance of events in one's life: "This happened to me." "I did this." "This is part of who I am." "This should not or will not disappear, and I act to preserve it by turning it to words and shaping them as story."

Related to the project of reclaiming one's experience is the project of speaking aloud what has been silenced by self or other. When Roethke wrote "My Papa's Waltz" in 1947, it may well have been the first instance of an alcoholic father being directly addressed and confronted in a lyric poem. Ever since the Romantics, the personal lyric has been reclaiming territory from the silence of family or social oppression: speaking what is taboo. This project validates and restabilizes the poet's self, but it also gives hope and courage to numerous readers who see their own experience dramatized in the poet's story.

Sometimes the agony of experience is so intense and threatening to the very existence of the self that, after the experience has been physically survived, story must circle back and revive the self spiritually and emotionally by retelling/reliving the experience as language in a poem. There are human experiences, too many of them, where the violence against the self is so intense that to simply retell them as chronology involves enormous courage and represents a self's triumph over that which threatens destruction. Here is a poem by the young American poet Michelle Wrybeck where the terror of an emergency medical procedure is described:

A Lesser Chaos

> In its zig-zagged scrawl
> the cardiac monitor reminds me why I am
> here on this see-through walled floor.
> Lights from my machines punctuate the darkness
> like stars. Gliding down the hallway
> the nurses move as if made of foam,
> bobbing from room to room on midnight
> rounds. Mine carries a flashlight,
> its beam slicing through my room
> like the blade of a sickle.
> The monitor's blip-blip bounces me alert
> and I watch the signature of my heart trail off
> into a long thin line.
>
> Alarms, alarms.
> A nurse wheels in

a crash cart, another
draws a syringe,
a third calibrates
my pumps. A doctor
cups my heel in his hand, bangs
his knuckles on my foot
to get a vein to rise.
Someone smears gel
on my torso and the overhead
light blares in its brilliant
white voice. I am dissolving
in its glare when two
surface pacemakers shock my chest,
send spasms through my breasts
that wrest me from the mattress
again and again until the screen
attests to my heart's rhythmic gestures.

And then the procession files out—
the carts, poles and consoles,
the medical personnel. Reflected
in the glass, a lesser chaos—my pulse
tracing itself in green moonlight.

By telling his or her story, the poet overcomes isolation and silence. Sometimes, stories allow the poet to make contact with lost
aspects of his or her own self. When we have forgotten or repressed
our own stories, or failed to value them enough to give them shape
and form, we are diminished beings. The telling of stories overcomes
this emotional self-alienation and releases emotion that has become
locked in our experience. The more of our own stories that we can
tell, the richer and more complex our selves become. The richer
a use we make of our past experiences, the more open we are to
present experience.

Expressing the Inexpressible: The Power of Symbol

The symbol gives rise to thought.
PAUL RICOEUR

Story aspires to act through to resolution, and its details, gestures, and actions are revealing and also symbolic. But often the action of story arrives at a dead end and cannot deliver on its promise to resolve conflicts. It is then that symbol appears spontaneously to incarnate those contradictions or conflicts in a single object. A symbol allows an object to mean more than itself, to take on additional meanings, as a magnet might bristle with paperclips. The symbol's unitary nature as an object acts as an embodiment of contraries and a reconciliation of thematic conflicts. Let me give an example from a poem by the African American poet Robert Hayden:

Those Winter Sundays

Sundays too my father got up early
and put his clothes on in the blueblack cold,
then with cracked hands that ached
from labor in the weekday weather made
banked fires blaze. No one ever thanked him.

I'd wake and hear the cold splintering, breaking.
When the rooms were warm, he'd call,
and slowly I would rise and dress,
fearing the chronic angers of that house,

Speaking indifferently to him,
who had driven out the cold
and polished my good shoes as well.
What did I know, what did I know
of love's austere and lonely offices?

The poem's two characters, father and son, exist in a state of tension. Each character's actions develop a separate thematic thread: the father's ceaseless labor, the son's fearful and guilty avoidance of his father. These separate stories are brought together and embodied

in the "good shoes," which become the single point of contact between the two characters who move about the dark house avoiding
each other. What sort of discordant or conflicting meanings are
concentrated in these shoes? They are the "good shoes," as opposed
to the everyday shoes. They are intended to be worn to church. The
father has polished them and left them, like an offering at a church
altar, for the son to wear. In order to go to church, the son must
put on the shoes and thus acknowledge the father and the father's
labor on his behalf—the shoes contain both the father's thankless
and dutiful labor and the son's guilty anguish. The son, who cannot
(he fears "the chronic angers of that house") or will not confront the
father, is forced to confront him indirectly in the shoes. Hayden's
poem starts as lyric story, narrows its focus to the intense tension of
symbol, and then breaks into an agonized and incantatory lament
("What did I know, what did I know?") as a way of resolving the
unresolvable misery of the poem.

The Irish poet William Butler Yeats, who was a master of symbols,
spoke about multiplicity within unity when he praised "ancient
symbols" (i.e., traditional symbols): "It is only by ancient symbols, by
symbols that have numberless meanings besides the one or two the
writer lays emphasis upon, or the half-score he knows of, that any
highly subjective art can escape from the barrenness and shallowness
of a too conscious arrangement, into the abundance and depth of
Nature" ("The Philosophy of Shelley's Poetry"). In this passage,
Yeats touches on a mysterious quality of symbols. Symbols can order
the conflicts within a poem (including the tension of disorder and
order) by concretely presenting them in a single, physical object, but
that object continues to suggest meanings beyond those consciously
intended by the poet. Meanings in symbol are like the twenty circus
clowns emerging from a tiny car, and we are well advised to yield to
the naive wonder of such abundance. Yet all the meanings do not and
cannot emerge; they lurk still in the object/symbol, refusing to give
up all their mystery to our need for understanding and explanation.
The ancient Athenians were polytheists with public shrines to all
their major gods, but they took no chances and also had a shrine

dedicated to "the unknown god" so as not to neglect some god whose presence and significance their limited understanding could not detect and name. Discussions of symbols should have a similar wary modesty: we cannot unlock all the mysteries, even those we think we ourselves have created.

Here's a poem by the contemporary American poet David Ignatow:

The Bagel

> I stopped to pick up the bagel
> rolling away in the wind,
> annoyed with myself
> for having dropped it
> as it were a portent.
> Faster and faster it rolled,
> with me running after it
> bent low, gritting my teeth,
> and I found myself doubled over
> and rolling down the street
> head over heels, one complete somersault
> after another like a bagel
> and strangely happy with myself.

In the poem's story, the dropping of the bagel is a "portent"—an omen, a sign of some larger significance. What does the bagel in this story signify? What does it symbolize? Hard to say, but we can start by noticing things about the poem. For one thing, the bagel is something completely other than the self, the "I" of the poem. The I is rather miserable: annoyed with himself, gritting his teeth. He cannot gracefully cope with even the minor disorder of his having dropped the bagel. Yet this little accident has the power to change the speaker's life, even to transform him from an upright, uptight stick figure into a round and rolling (and rollicking) object much like a bagel. He has become the bagel he pursues; he has also, in the process, become inexplicably transformed emotionally: "strangely happy" with himself.

The speaker of Ignatow's poem is very different from Neruda's speaker in "Ode to My Socks." In that poem, the speaker is wide open to the curious delight of the ordinary (the socks), and his flurry of wild metaphors enacts his exuberant responsiveness. Ignatow's speaker is closed-up and angry; he has no spontaneous and intimate access to the transforming powers of metaphor. Ignatow's is an odd tale: unless I become as a bagel, I shall not be free. An odd symbol of freedom and release from the self (this rolling circle of boiled and baked dough). Obviously, one of Lawrence's three strange angels nudged his elbow and made him drop the bagel. You must be lost, in order to be found. You must lose your balance (bending over to grab a rolling bagel), in order to regain your (spiritual and emotional) stability.

Yeats tells us that "ancient symbols" have more meanings locked in them than the poet can realize, but Ignatow's poem tells us something else. Surely, his bagel is not an "ancient symbol"—it was probably baked that day. But there is something about symbols in general that resists complete elucidation and translation into "meaning." A symbol *is* meaning.

Bearing the Unbearable: The Power of Incantation

In the two powers we've briefly explored, the poet's self is still in control of thematic material. But the lyric's third primal ordering power is capable of dealing with even more extreme disorderings, catastrophes so powerful that the self is unable to shape them toward the coherence of story or the complex concentration of symbol. With incantation, the self discovers that it can be sustained, if all else fails, through rhythmic repetition alone. In these instances, incantation is like a woven raft of sound on which the self floats above the floodwaters of chaos.

Holman and Harmon's *Handbook to Literature* (1992) defines incantation as follows: "A formulaic use of language, usually spoken or chanted, either to create intense emotional effects or to produce magical results." This definition links emotional power, magic, and the incantatory repetition of sounds and phrases, although it also indicates the handbook's notion that poetry is a series of calculated effects to manipulate an audience. In line with our view of the survival function of the personal lyric, I would add that incantation is used to *express* intense emotions as well as to create them. That is, I want to honor the poet's authentic survival project first and his or her intended effect on an audience second.

Incantation is the most primitive (and powerful) of linguistic forms. We encounter it constantly in tribal poetries. It also appears spontaneously in the rhythmic moans of grief and orgasm, lament and ecstasy. Each of these situations might erupt in a single shout, but they are equally likely to bring forth the rhythmic moan of incantation: Molly Bloom's repeated "yes" of sexual surrender and affirmation that culminates Joyce's *Ulysses* (" . . . and then I asked him with my eyes again yes and then he asked me would I yes to say yes my mountain flower and first I put my arms around him yes and drew him down to me so he could feel my breasts all perfume yes and his heart was going like mad and yes I said yes I will Yes") or King Lear's agonized groans over his dead daughter: "Never, never, never, never, never . . ."

Incantation as expression and as consolation. Anyone who has cried deeply in his or her life knows that there is a certain point at which sobbing takes on a rhythmic pattern, and that this stage of weeping has about it something that soothes the weeper. It is the power of incantation at work. A griever might, in the same way, repeat a loved name over and over. And elegies are full of incantatory repetitions, with their power to ease suffering. How much mysterious solace emerges from incantatory repetition. How little from silent grieving, or the piercing, shapeless cry of despair.

Survival and the consoling power of repeated sounds. It's even there, almost ridiculously, in the spontaneous response when you hit your thumb with a hammer: you might shout, "Ow!" but you are just as likely to shout, "Ow, ow, ow, ow!" because there is something oddly satisfying and sustaining in that repetition.

Almost all magical spells are based in such rhythms. Think of the rich repetitiveness of "Abracadabra" or the witches' chant from *Macbeth*: "Double, double, toil and trouble / Fire burn and cauldron bubble." Rhyme itself might be best understood as a subtler form of incantation whose ordering power is prized even when it is not connected to the powerful emotions we have just considered.

EARLY IN THE nineteenth century, Coleridge claimed there were only two things a poet must have in order to become a poet. One of them concerned that interplay of sounds that Coleridge called "musical delight" and spoke of in this way: "the sense of musical delight, with the power of producing it." Musical delight is another way of talking about rhythm and the repetition and variation of sounds.

Coleridge himself was richly endowed with this gift, and these opening lines of his poem "Kubla Khan" are among the most memorable lines of any poem in English precisely because of their incantatory power:

> In Xanadu did Kubla Khan
> A stately Pleasure Dome decree.

The opening line alone is dense with internal rhyme and sound patterning: du/Ku, Xan/Khan, alliterations of "d" and "n," and the vowel rhyme of short "a" sounds. It might seem that Coleridge's poem connects incantation to musical delight and that pleasure is far from the question of the self's survival, but not necessarily. In the poem's narrative, Kubla Khan builds a wall around an area to create a safe space in which to construct his pleasure dome. He is, in fact, trying to construct an earthly paradise. The word "paradise" is itself of Arabic origin and means "a walled garden." Such walled gardens in a desert culture were places where privileged people could enjoy greenery, fountains, and shade. But this paradisal, ordered space is haunted by a disorder that penetrates its walls:

> And 'mid this tumult Kubla heard from far
> Ancestral voices prophesying war.

The poem then shifts from a narrative about Kubla to the speaker, who goes on to claim that *he* himself has the power to create that pleasure dome out of words ("That with music loud and long, / I would build that dome in air"). In short, the poem lays claim to the magical powers of rhythmical, incantatory language and links them to sustaining delight:

> For he on honey-dew hath fed
> And drunk the milk of Paradise.

But incantatory language can protect us as well from even deeper eruptions of disorder, as in William Blake's poem "The Tyger":

> Tyger! Tyger! burning bright
> In the forests of the night,
> What immortal hand or eye
> Could frame thy fearful symmetry?
>
> In what distant deeps or skies
> Burnt the fire of thine eyes?
> On what wings dare he aspire?
> What the hand dare seize the fire?
>
> And what shoulder, & what art,
> Could twist the sinews of thy heart?
> And when thy heart began to beat,
> What dread hand? & what dread feet?
>
> What the hammer? what the chain?
> In what furnace was thy brain?
> What the anvil? what dread grasp
> Dare its deadly terrors clasp?
>
> When the stars threw down their spears,
> And water'd heaven with their tears,
> Did he smile his work to see?
> Did he who made the Lamb make thee?
>
> Tyger! Tyger! burning bright
> In the forests of the night,
> What immortal hand or eye
> Dare frame thy fearful symmetry?

The tiger's "fearful symmetry" (its frightening, flamelike stripes of orange and black) prompts the poet to wonder how such a creature fits into the order of nature and religion: who could have created such a fierce and terrifying beast? The same God who made lambs? Who made Christ, the Lamb of God? The tiger's existence represents the dynamic presence of violence and destruction in the world. It shows that nature is not all flowers and rainbows. And the appearance of the tiger in this poem is an explosion of violence into the ordering of poetry. Can it be accommodated? Can it be ordered?

Of course, in an elegant visual/physical sense, the tiger is already ordered: his coat is *symmetrical*, he is marked and made remarkable by the balanced order of design. But any reassurance this patterned symmetry might inspire is undercut by the animal's "fearful" nature: this is a clawed, powerful carnivore stalking the dark, nighttime jungle (and the forest/jungle itself is an image of awesome disorder).

What else then, beyond the visual symmetry of the tiger's pelt, orders Blake's poem? Formally, of course, the ordering of rhyme and repeated stanzas. But finally I would say that Blake's strongest ordering strategy is the decision to "frame" the poem with nearly identical first and last stanzas—this is a very noticeable formal patterning (a *symmetry* in fact) that Blake presents in the absence of any major thematic ordering.

That is to say, the poem cannot or does not answer the disturbing questions it asks throughout the poem. In fact, those insistent questions actually *raise* the level of intensity, since the poem itself offers no answers to its own questions and, for that matter, few probably come to the reader's mind as she or he reads. Ultimately, it is the framing symmetry of the repeated first and last stanzas (i.e., incantation) that sustains the poem against the profound turbulence it has conjured up.

In the following Polynesian lament, chronology moves inevitably toward the overwhelming dissolutions of old age and impending death as the poem enumerates and celebrates the incidents of a shared life:

Alas! We grow old, O beloved,
We two.

We two indeed together, O beloved,
When we two were little
When we played together in the sea.

We two indeed together, O beloved,
When we took our walks together
As we were growing up.

We two indeed together, O beloved,
When your breasts were firm and round,
When your breasts drooped in motherhood.

We two indeed together, O beloved,
When your hair floated down your back,
When your body was strong and virile.

We two indeed together, O beloved,
When our bodies grew old and thin,
Like a flat-fish resting on the bottom.

We two indeed together, O beloved,
When so feeble we but sat apart,
So feeble we could but rest the hours away.

We two indeed together, O beloved,
When our dim eyes gaze at the misty skies,
When vision fails to see their splendour.
Ah, whither does God draw me?
(from *The Unwritten Song*, ed. Trask, 2:91)

Against the declines and quiet terrors of the last three stanzas, the poem marshals the powerful counterforce of its incantatory phrase "we two indeed together." In this insistent phrase, we hear how joys and miseries that have been shared rather than endured alone are more bearable.

Certainly, one of the most unbearable instances of destructive violence in Western history was the Holocaust. There are many who feel that against the horror of such evil, nothing can be affirmed and the best response is the stunned silence of acknowledgment. These people feel that to attempt any affirmation against so vast and intentional a destructiveness would be obscene. But such thinking ignores the fact that the human spirit must affirm itself against the agonies it undergoes and that the personal lyric's task is to attempt ordering affirmations even against such overwhelming evil. Of course, the reality and force of so potent an evil silences almost all imaginable thematic affirmations, and it is possible that incantation alone has the power to suspend us above such an abyss. Remember, incantation's sustaining power is primarily formal (the repeating formal pattern of sounds) and thus is not necessarily tied to content. An answer or response to the Holocaust that attempted to affirm something to do with content would be a difficult or even impossible task for any poet.

One of the few poems that people have considered to possess the dignity and power necessary for the subject of the Holocaust is Paul Celan's poem "Deathfugue." Celan (1920–1970) was the son of parents who disappeared into Nazi extermination camps, which he himself narrowly escaped. His poem organizes itself around insistent incantation from the very beginning, a structuring John Felstiner's translation preserves:

> Black milk of daybreak we drink it at evening
> we drink it at midday and morning we drink it at night
>   we drink and we drink.

And each of its four stanzas begins with this incantation. We can note that "black milk" is a symbolic image and seems to concentrate the tension of something life-sustaining and essential (milk) transformed into something sinisterly magical and repellent (black milk). But the power of sustaining the self against the horror rests with the incantatory repetition and its repeated action: "We drink and we drink." The action of drinking this weird liquid sounds as if it is both chosen by the self as the only way to survive and also forced on the self as a punishment. This grim paradox haunts the poem and cannot be overcome. All it can do (and this is a great deal) is make the unbearable bearable, as it must be if the human spirit is to be kept alive in its house of embodiment.

PART TWO

Trauma and Transformation

CHAPTER EIGHT

The Dangerous Angel

The gods I created from my sweat but mankind is from the tears of my eye.

The "Universal Lord," in the Egyptian *Book of Three Ways*

According to Genesis 32, Jacob encountered a "man" on the banks of the Jabok River. This "man" was almost certainly a supernatural creature whom God had sent. Jacob and the stranger fought all night, wrestling in a violent and intimate embrace. At a certain point, his antagonist touched Jacob's thigh and threw his hip out of joint, but Jacob held on until the creature demanded to be freed because day was breaking. "I will not let you go unless you bless me," Jacob replied. And the creature did bless him and gave him a new name, "Israel," because, he said, "You have striven with God and with men and have prevailed."

In a sense, Jacob wrestled with the unfathomable mystery of existence in its darkest form—the mystery of unprovoked violence and evil. A mystery that sought to destroy him but that, when resisted heroically, could be transformed into a sort of blessing.

It might seem odd, even offensive to use the word blessing in proximity to the terrors of traumatic violence. But "blessing" itself is a strange word. In French *blesser* is a verb meaning "to wound." "Blessing" in modern English is the bestowal of spiritual grace and power through a gesture. Often, in the Christian ceremony of baptism, this gesture involves the sprinkling of water on the person. But the original Anglo-Saxon origin of blessing is *blestein*, which meant "to spatter with blood." The history of the word itself enacts an uncanny overlapping of violence, wounding, and spiritual grace, as if it wishes to hint at some connection deeper than logic can penetrate.

Often, as a survivor of trauma, I wonder: why did I survive? How could I have stood so close to the scene of violence as to have been spattered with blood (and for some survivors of trauma, the blood was their own)? How could I have been that close and not been destroyed by it? Why was I spared? Why am I still alive? These questions, which are unanswerable, have the power to initiate a quest for meanings and purpose.

But this quest born out of trauma doesn't simply lead the survivor forward. First it leads him or her backward, back to the scene of the trauma where the struggle must take place with the demon or angel who incarnates the mystery of violence and the mystery of rebirth and transformation. (We might think of this angel as the *duende* described in Federico García Lorca's brief essay: a demonic presence his beloved Andalusian gypsies felt was essential to any important art, from poetry to flamenco dance to bullfighting. Without *duende*, poetry could be beautiful, but it could not transform the soul.) Wrestling such a creature, we may, if we prevail, receive its blessing: a new name, a new self, a new purpose.

Trauma and the Shattering of Self

I can connect
Nothing with nothing.
T. S. ELIOT, *The Waste Land*

Trauma is a Greek word meaning "wound." In medicine, it usually refers to bodily injury caused by violence or some other external agent, and in psychiatry it refers to any startling incident that has a lasting effect on our mental life. The kinds of events that can precipitate trauma vary enormously, though some occur with disheartening frequency. Among the most explored causes of trauma in American culture are sexual assault against women and children and, among men, prolonged exposure to heavy combat. The latter diagnosis has become familiar to us as the post-traumatic stress disorder that emerged into public notice after the

Vietnam War. But trauma can also be caused by family and urban violence; by natural disasters such as earthquakes, tornadoes, and floods; and by mere proximity to sudden deaths. These experiences are profound and destructive manifestations of disorder that challenge some of our most basic beliefs. As Judith Herman puts it in her remarkable book *Trauma and Recovery* (1991), "To study psychological trauma is to come face to face both with human vulnerability in the natural world and with the capacity for evil in human nature" (7).

For the purposes of our discussion of trauma and poetry, nothing could be more pertinent than Herman's description of how a traumatized self inhabits a world totally dominated and devastated by alienation and despair:

> Traumatic events call into question basic human relationships. They breach the attachments of family, friendship, love, and community. They shatter the construction of the self that is formed and sustained in relation to others. They undermine the belief systems that give meaning to human experience. They violate the victim's faith in a natural or divine order and cast the victim into a state of existential crisis. (51)

Cut off from all connections and meaning schemes, how can the self survive? Herman discusses at length the ways in which the guilt, shame, doubt, and sense of helplessness that assail the trauma victim threaten to utterly abolish the self's developmental quest for autonomy and self-assurance. In addition, the most extreme cases of trauma leave the victim open to sudden eruptions of long-past agony into a present moment, what we've come to refer to as "flashbacks." These eruptions strike with enormous and debilitating power; a power that Emily Dickinson images as a lightning storm that refuses to cease, even though, by definition, "storm" is brief and must end:

> It struck me – every Day—
> The Lightning was as new
> As if the Cloud that instant slit
> And let the Fire through—

It burned Me – in the Night –
It Blistered to My Dream –
It sickened fresh upon my sight –
With every Morn that came –

I thought that storm – was brief
The Maddest – quickest by –
But Nature lost the Date of This –
And left it in the Sky. (J. 362)

Judith Herman examines the ways in which trauma victims can recover through prolonged therapy and support groups. I would add to these more recent methods the ancient method of composing or reciting personal lyrics as a means by which individuals can overcome the destructive powers of trauma. The poet who translates her "storm" into language and dramatizes it will have taken a first, strong step toward healing.

Trauma and Radical Freedom

Sometimes hell is a good place—if it proves to one that because it exists, so must its opposite, heaven, exist. And what was heaven? Poetry.

GREGORY CORSO

When I write a poem to help myself cope with a serious disturbance, I do so by registering the disorder that first destabilized me and then incorporating it into the poem. The literary result is the poem of survival. The psychological result is a more flexible and comprehensive self. But what about those situations in which trauma can't be assimilated in the ordinary sense of the word? What about those cases of extreme desolation in which all connections between self and outer world are snapped, along with those connecting the self to its inner life, *and* the very integrity and coherence of the self is profoundly shaken?

It is precisely in such bleak and hopeless-seeming circumstances that the personal lyric proposes its hope. The very hopelessness of the shattered self is its hope, because this devastated self possesses a radical *freedom*. All the ordinary, sustaining eros-connections to the world have been torn: the web is in shreds. The self is therefore free to make new connections to the world. And it has an even more primary task and opportunity: to make a new self. To create a new self to inhabit this new world (or this old world of "new" connections).

What certain poets of trauma intuit is that their old self cannot survive the suffering it has experienced without succumbing. Thus *necessity* permits and compels imagination to create a new self, a self strong enough or different enough to move *through* and *beyond* the trauma and its aftermath.

The Iroquois and the Flying Heads

Among the Iroquois Indian tribes of the Northeast, the fiercest and most dangerous supernatural creatures were called "flying heads"—demons in the form of disembodied heads that zoomed at night among the trees, their faces distorted with the anguish of evil and malice. If you saw one in a dream, you had to go into the woods, carve its features on a living basswood tree, then, with appropriate rituals, cut down the tree, take the carved section home and continue carving until you had a completed mask that replicated the demon's face. Possession of such a mask (and the ordeal and rituals it signified) qualified you for membership in the False Face Society. Donning your mask in False Face ceremonies, you and your fellow members visited the ill and afflicted and had the power to cure certain diseases. All these shamanic healing affiliations and their social status were yours, if you made the mask that corresponded to the demon who had appeared in your dream. If you ignored the dream or failed to respond to it by making the mask, you yourself would sicken and die.

The Iroquois anecdote has some striking parallels with the creative (i.e., poem-writing) response to individual trauma. The artifact the dreamer makes is a mask depicting the terrifying demon, which is analogous to "saying the unsayable" in psychological trauma—telling what happened to you, what you saw with your own eyes. *But* this mask-making is also an act of creating a new face for the self, a "new self." Paradoxically, when the dreamer puts on this mask, he does not also put on the assaultive and destructive power of the demon, he does not "become" the demon. Quite the opposite. Something in the carving process and its attendant rituals has transformed this demonic energy into something positive, so that when the dreamer puts on the mask his new identity is animated by positive, healing energy. This is more than the simple "mastery of what threatened to master you" discussed in the chapters on survival; this is transformative of both the self and the destructive power that assailed the self.

Wearing his mask, the dreamer has a new identity and a new power that lead him to a new purpose: to help heal others. He has gained membership in a community of healers who have undergone similar traumas and recovered. Their actions and responses have transformed them (they each have a different mask, the mask of their own demon) and given them the power to help others. Thus the dreamer who was isolated and alienated by the traumatic dream has become reconnected to other people and now inhabits a meaningful, purposeful world. The dreamer who has successfully followed this process of transformation has emerged far stronger than he began. He is a new person in a new world.

The Poet, the Shaman, and the Shattered Self

No man is an island, entire of itself; every man is a piece
of the continent, a part of the main.
JOHN DONNE, "Meditation XVII"

Because of the transformative power of shamanism, it might be worth a quick glance at the phenomenon before we return to the story of trauma and poetry. In numerous tribal cultures, the shaman is a healer. To become a shaman is not so much a choice as it is a consequence of catastrophic personal experience that is then embraced and engaged as a life-path. What sets someone on a shamanic path is an early experience of near-death or some severe, involuntary affliction. In the belief system of the tribal societies where shamanism flourishes, when someone is sick or dying their soul has left his or her body and traveled to the Land of the Dead. Once the soul takes up residence there, the mortal body dies. When someone is very ill or struck down by some fit, vision, or nervous collapse, her soul begins that journey. Some unusual people recover from these experiences despite the odds, and these people return from the land of the dead with a new power: the power to go there and return more or less at will. This extraordinary power is often accessed through dance, trance states, and the singing of power songs (poems) that record and facilitate the supernatural journey. These people now have a social function: as shamans, they can attend sick people and, through their trance journeys, save them by traveling to the land of the dead and bringing back their departed souls.

The shaman, like our contemporary trauma victim, has been cut off from the rest of the social community by a personal experience of violent destructiveness. He could have died; he could have lived in a post-traumatic state of complete despair and alienation, but instead he responded creatively and courageously by engaging the destructive force and transforming it and himself at the same time.

Keats's Poet and Dreaming Thing

What benefit canst thou do, or all thy tribe
To the great world? Thou art a dreaming thing,
A fever of thyself.

JOHN KEATS, *Hyperion: A Vision*

Unlike the shaman in a traditional society, who is trained and guided by tradition and by others in his profession and supported by social context, the poet of trauma and transformation must often struggle alone and without any compass. Though Keats knew nothing of shamanism and no contemporary theories of poetry validated his vision, his struggle to understand his purpose as a poet led him to intuit the profound link between trauma and the ability to heal and console others who suffer.

In 1819, about a year before his terrible illness caused him to cease writing entirely, Keats began a long, unfinished narrative called *Hyperion: A Vision*. A short way into the poem, the speaker is challenged by a female spirit who presides over a ruined temple altar. The spirit seems to know who the speaker is, and the speaker responds: "What am I then: thou spakest of my tribe: / What tribe?" We learn that the spirit has mistaken Keats for a dreamer rather than a poet. Such a mistake is easy to make she says, since they are both *very* similar (alienated and awakened) and *very* different in temperament and response:

> Art thou not of the dreamer tribe?
> The poet and the dreamer are distinct,
> Diverse, sheer opposite, antipodes.
> The one pours out a balm upon the world,
> The other vexes it.

And here we are at the heart of the individual, transformative response to trauma. The "dreamer" is a traumatized self, bearing all the marks of dissociation Judith Herman has outlined: guilt, alienation, disconnection from the world and from others. The dreamer "venoms all his days / Bearing more woe than all his sins deserve" (ll. 175–76). He suffers the agony and forlornness of his trauma without any respite or solution. By contrast, the poet is a "physician to all men." That the spirit can be fooled as to Keats's speaker's true identity is a sign that they *are*, in a sense, each other. Or rather, they are the same self in two different modes: traumatized and transformed. The Keats who was a deeply damaged "dreamer" has become a "poet" and physician (or shaman) whose songs and poems are "a balm" and healing medicine for those who hear them.

Nor should we forget that Keats himself was a serious medical student before he became obsessed with poetry, and so the metaphor of poet as physician had reality for him. In a further, uncanny link between shamanism and Keats's poem, the female spirit announces that Keats's protagonist has also undergone the near-death experience that allows shamans to gain their spiritual healing power:

> Thou hast felt
> What 'tis to die and live again before
> Thy fated hour.

Culture-Wide Trauma and the Lyric Poet

Besides the quasi-shamanic model Keats posits, there are other ways in which the personal-lyric poet can connect to the surrounding human community by means of his or her own transformative encounter with trauma. For one thing, not all trauma is individual. Or, we could say, destructive violence can be individual in impact, yet so widespread as to devastate whole societies. Obvious examples include war, genocide, riots, natural disasters, famines, and epidemics. In addition, certain kinds of traumatic violence are so pervasive, such as racially motivated violence, violence against gays and lesbians, and sexual assault against women, that they resonate within the culture as a whole.

Totalitarian regimes that practice systemic violence and terror against their own citizens have punctuated the twentieth century with mass trauma. The Soviet regime presided over by Joseph Stalin terrorized an entire society as well as many poets. One of them, Anna Akhmatova, was one of the greatest Russian lyric poets of the twentieth century. She mostly wrote personal lyrics about the torments of passionate love, and the early work that made her famous had no political content whatsoever. But she also lived most of her life in Stalin's police state, and her status as a great poet gave her no immunity from harassment and the homicidal depredations of the Gulag system. Although she herself escaped direct annihilation, her husband was arrested and shot by the secret police and her beloved son was imprisoned. At the height of the Yezhov terror (1937–38), hundreds of thousands of innocent Russian citizens were tortured and sent to Siberian labor camps to slave and die.

One of many diabolical aspects of Stalin's police state was its policy of arresting people, throwing them in prison, and then providing no further information to their loved ones as to their fate. Akhmatova, like many others, had no way of knowing whether her son was still being kept in the Leningrad prison into which he had disappeared, nor if he was even still alive. Along with thousands of other relatives, mostly mothers, she stood each dawn in a long line outside the Leningrad prison with a package and a bribe, waiting for her chance to present it to the guards. But of course, the guards accepted her bribes and packages without comment and so she learned nothing about her son and the whole process was hopeless.

From her experience outside the prison and the other violent losses she suffered, she fashioned a long lyric sequence entitled "Requiem." In a note preceding the poem, she speaks of how it came into being:

In the terrible years of the Yezhov terror I spent seventeen months in line outside the prison in Leningrad. One day somebody identified me. Standing behind me was a woman, with lips blue from the cold, who had, of course, never heard me called by name before. Now she started out of the torpor common to us all and asked me in a whisper (everyone whispered there): "Can you describe this?" And I said: "I can." Then something like a smile passed fleetingly over what had been her face.

Not only can Akhmatova say the unsayable (here, it is unsayable because to say it she would risk imprisonment, torture, and death), but she can and does become a voice for the voiceless. She does so, not by attempting to adopt a generalized voice of suffering, but instead by writing a linked series of personal lyrics about her own traumatic losses. In the process of articulating her own griefs, she also dramatizes the analogous suffering of hundreds of thousands of her fellow citizens. What others registered as mute, brute violence, Akhmatova was able to transform into the language of a spirit determined to survive. Her poem could not be printed anywhere in Russia until well after Stalin's death, but that did not prevent it from spreading in handwritten copies and by word of mouth until it was known by heart by thousands of Russians.

Relearning the Language, Rebuilding the World

During the Second World War, 6.3 million Poles died out of a prewar population of about 10 million. Of those dead, 5.7 million were civilians, and, of those, 3 million were Jews (*The People's Almanac Presents the Twentieth Century*, 208). It is impossible to imagine that many among those who survived escaped the trauma and suffering of living in these times. The Polish people were inconceivably devastated by this destruction.

One of the major Polish poets to emerge from the war was Tadeusz Rozewicz, who published his first collection, *The Survivor*, when he was still in his twenties, shortly after the war's end. Rozewicz was a member of the guerrilla Home Army and was deeply traumatized by what he had seen and done during the war. Although he wished to be a poet, he felt a genuine hatred for poetry's traditional concern with "beauty" and was determined to create an "anti-poetry." This anti-poetry, stripped of all ornament and poetical devices like rhyme, meter, and metaphor, would struggle to be adequate to what he had seen, felt, and done rather than contaminate itself with the complacent "lies" of beauty and harmony.

With astonishingly simple eloquence, Rozewicz dramatizes his post-apocalyptic struggle to create a new self and a new world of meaning after massive devastation. The poem's opening lines, with the speaker "lost" in the middle of his life, echo one of the greatest Western visionary poems of despair, confusion, and renewal, Dante's *Divine Comedy*:

In the Middle of Life

After the end of the world
after my death

I found myself in the middle of life
I created myself
constructed life
people animals landscapes

this is a table I was saying
this is a table
on the table are lying bread a knife
the knife serves to cut the bread
people nourish themselves with bread

one should love man
I was learning by night and day
what one should love
I answered man

this is a window I was saying
this is a window
beyond the window is a garden
in the garden I see an apple tree
the apple tree blossoms
the blossoms fall off
the fruits take form
they ripen my father is picking up an apple
that man who is picking up an apple
is my father
I was sitting on the threshold of the house

that old woman who
is pulling a goat on a rope
is more necessary
and more precious
than the seven wonders of the world
whoever thinks and feels
that she is not necessary
he is guilty of genocide

this is a man
this is a tree this is bread

people nourish themselves in order to live
I was repeating to myself
human life is important
human life has great importance
the value of life
surpasses the value of all the objects
which man has made
man is a great treasure
I was repeating stubbornly

this is water I was saying
I was stroking the waves with my hand
and conversing with the river
water I said
good water
this is I

the man talked to the water
talked to the moon
to the flowers to the rain
he talked to the earth
to the birds
to the sky

the sky was silent
the earth was silent
if he heard a voice
which flowed
from the earth from the water from the sky
it was the voice of another man.

Rozewicz's "I" rebuilds both world and self *with* and *through* language. The poem is, among other things, a language primer: a first reading book for a "child" or a shell-shocked, traumatized veteran who must relearn everything from scratch and through elementary incantatory repetitions: "this is a man / this is a tree this is bread." It's as if Rozewicz was the blind Helen Keller learning to "see" through language, only Rozewicz has been blinded by violence and evil. His learning to see again through words involves the identification of things (connecting nouns to objects, to concrete, particular things), but the speaker must also learn or relearn purposes. What is an object for? What purpose does it serve? These simple objects connect to basic needs:

> on the table are lying bread a knife
> the knife serves to cut the bread
> people nourish themselves with bread

Behind this simple connection and affirmation of a knife slicing bread lurks the sinister other purpose for knives: to cut and kill people. What might seem a simple relearning is also an *unlearning* of traumatic violence in order to reestablish a stable, moral world.

There is a heartbreaking desire to affirm that the physical world of nature is innocent, as if any garden could be Eden before the Fall:

> this is a window I was saying
> this is a window
> beyond the window is a garden
> in the garden I see an apple tree
> the apple tree blossoms
> the blossoms fall off
> the fruits take form
> they ripen my father is picking up an apple
> that man who is picking up an apple
> is my father

And as if the safe and natural rhythms of the Edenic garden, once attested, can be extended to include known human beings ("my father . . . that man . . . is my father") whose familial connection makes them less dangerous. Gradually the frame of affirmative reference expands to include unrelated and unaggressive other humans ("that old woman").

This world that the poet is "stubbornly" building up or rebuilding with his repetitious phrases and simple words must place enormous value on each individual human being if it is to have any hope of reestablishing sustaining relationships in a world that has been annihilated by mass, undiscriminating violence:

> that old woman who
> is pulling a goat on a rope
> is more necessary
> and more precious
> than the seven wonders of the world
> whoever thinks and feels
> that she is not necessary
> he is guilty of genocide

To fail to recognize and insist on the infinite intrinsic worth of individuals is, according to Rozewicz's poem, to be complicit with a genocidal mind-set, the same mind-set that has so recently resulted in "the end of the world." In Rozewicz's new world, people must not abstract away from embodiment and concrete reality, must not become detached from the physical world for fear that they will once again fall prey to the murderous ideologies that underlie genocide.

Although Rozewicz's traumatized, "posthumous" poet is arriving at his tentative affirmations about life by way of objects (knives and bread, apple trees and goats), his ultimate and necessary goal is to reconnect with human beings (father, old woman) and finally to assert the central role of other human beings in any affirmative scheme:

> I was repeating to myself
> human life is important
> human life has great importance
> the value of life
> surpasses the value of all the objects
> which man has made

In this new or renewed world, objects are far less important than people. A relationship with the natural world is imagined and affirmed: "the man talked to the water / talked to the moon." But it is still the *human* response, the bond between self and other self that constitutes the poem's final assertion and affirmation:

the sky was silent
the earth was silent
if he heard a voice
which flowed
from the earth from the water from the sky
it was the voice of another man.

SURELY, WE WOULD be right to say that trauma is, by definition, among the fiercest and most destructive forms disorder can take. Trauma, either on an intimate or a collective scale, has the power to annihilate the self and shred the web of meanings that supports its existence. And yet, the evidence of lyric poetry is equally clear— deep in the recesses of the human spirit, there is some instinct to rebuild the web of meanings with the same quiet determination we witness in the garden spider as it repairs the threads winds and weather have torn.

CHAPTER NINE

Convulsive Transformation of the Overculture

> I pray for many things, things the Overculture
> may never pray for.
> SARA HUTCHINSON

Sara Hutchinson is a Cherokee Indian woman inter-
viewed in the book *Surviving in Two Worlds*. The "two worlds" are
the worlds of contemporary, white-dominated America and the traditional world of first Americans. In the book, she does not define
the term "Overculture" quoted above, and so, in adopting it, I have
given it my own definition. In my definition, Overculture refers to
the ideological and institutional formations and attitudes that support a given society or culture—established religions and political,
social, and economic structures, as well as the values that validate
them or emerge from them. The Overculture, then, is the stream
that we individuals swim in. But unlike fish, individual humans can
dream: they can "pray for" other things and values than those they
inherit because of where and when they are born.

Not all culture-wide traumas can be neatly placed in a framework
of a few crucial years such as World War II or the Yeshov Terror
written about by Rozewicz and Akhmatova. The most significant
culture-wide convulsion in the Western world took place during
the eighteenth century. This isn't the place to do more than list
some of the turbulent phenomena that century unleashed, but they
are worth mentioning, since they form the context of our contemporary being and also explain why the personal lyric is so important
in our modern world.

Although the changes I refer to took place in all aspects of society, perhaps we could say they started in science with the seventeenth-century genius Isaac Newton. As few individuals have, Newton changed the world irrevocably. His discoveries concerning gravity, optics, and mathematics made it seem possible to understand the fundamental scientific laws that rule the entire material world. It's impossible to exaggerate the impact of his activities. As Alexander Pope put it in a deliberate parody of the Biblical creation story:

Nature and Nature's laws lay hid in night:
God said, "Let Newton be!" and all was light.

In the wake of these scientific breakthroughs came technology, the practical application of scientific principles to create inventions such as the steam engine and the spinning jenny, which, in turn, fed the growth of the industrial systems of emergent capitalism.

A century after Newton, his example inspired the Enlightenment intellectuals. Such thinkers as David Hume and Adam Smith in Scotland; Voltaire, Diderot, D'Alembert, Montesquieu, and others in France; Kant in Germany; and Jefferson, Franklin, and Madison in America were eager to use reason and rationality to make sense of the human world, either deductively (as in mathematics) or inductively (as in physics). Progress would replace superstition and hide-bound tradition. Using the rationality and logic Newton had employed so successfully in physics, they would redesign the intellectual, moral, and political universes as Newton had the scientific.

In England, which had undergone a bloody political revolution in the seventeenth century, there was sufficient political flexibility to permit the emerging bourgeoisie and capitalists to take leading roles in running the country. In France, on the other hand, the aristocrats and church hierarchy resisted the political implications of economic and intellectual changes, as did the king of France himself. This resistance met its end with the violent upheaval we know as the French Revolution, which itself metamorphosed into the Terror, whose ceaseless guillotinings presaged the state terrorisms of our own times.

Everything in Western Europe, especially England and France, was in transition. And toward what? No one knew. Of course, as always, people responded differently. Some were exhilarated and joined their fates to the movements and motions, gave themselves up to the new ideas and opportunities. But many others were confused and uncertain about the intense and ceaseless change that was overtaking and altering all that surrounded them in the physical and intellectual landscape. They felt the idea and belief structures they had been raised within crumbling under the pressures of new developments. Where would they turn for the ordering ideas and values that we call meaning? Many felt they could no longer rely on religion or philosophy. Nor was this existential crisis merely intellectual; people *felt* it, experienced it personally as anxiety, confusion, and despair. Forced to confront this bewildering world naked of inherited beliefs, individual selves fell back on their own world of feelings and experience. It is just such a set of crisis conditions that would bring the personal lyric to the fore as a central mode of meaning making.

Poetry Switches Sides

Until the mid-eighteenth century, most lyric poets either emerged from or worked for the Overculture, expressing and dramatizing the values and attitudes of the ruling elites. But in the mid-eighteenth century, as the Overculture began to change rapidly and chaotically, a number of poets "switched sides" and began to speak from other points of view besides that of the ruling classes.

No two poets could better illustrate divergent attitudes toward this moment of vast change than Alexander Pope (1688–1744), who maintained allegiance to the prevailing culture and ideals of his time, and William Blake (1757–1827), who worked outside and against the dominant culture. (Predictably, Blake differed profoundly from Pope in his response to Isaac Newton's work, feeling it trapped man in a mechanistic universe. According to Blake, imagination was the essential meaning-making power—it gave "double vision" and kept us from "single vision & Newton's sleep.")

Pope, who was a member of the upper middle class and identified with the ruling system in the England of his time, affirmed the status quo. It's not that Pope was a complete member of the ruling elite. For example, being raised a Roman Catholic in a country where Anglicanism was the established religion, Pope was legally excluded from the universities at Oxford and Cambridge and had to be educated at home by tutors. But Pope definitely felt himself to be on the side of order, resisting the chaos of change. According to the imaginative scheme Pope adopted to preserve and defend this order, individuals had to cooperate with the established and traditional political and religious hierarchical systems. In his long poem "Essay on Man," Pope set out to elaborate his scheme in rhymed couplets.

The order he perceives and urges is an order that asks individuals to adjust to "laws" and "rules": those of Nature and of society as well as those of God. According to Pope, they are all the same, all concentric. The individual must adjust, accept, submit. Here the poet rebukes the individual ("vile worm") who would, through his or her own needs or willfulness, disturb this delicate yet powerful cosmic and social order:

> The least confusion but in one, not all
> That system only, but the Whole must fall.
> Let earth unbalanced from her orbit fly,
> Planets and suns run lawless through the sky,
> Let ruling angels from their spheres be hurled,
> Being on being wrecked, and world on world,
> Heaven's whole foundations to their center nod,
> And Nature tremble to the throne of God:
> All this dread ORDER break—for whom? for thee?
> Vile worm!—oh, madness, pride, impiety!
> ("An Essay on Man," section 1, ll. 249–58)

Pope's order culminates in the pithy demand that the individual self submit and adjust to the status quo: "One truth is clear, WHATEVER IS, IS RIGHT."

But there's another way to look at the mathematically precise social ordering Pope celebrates: it can be seen and felt as oppressive. William Blake, the great pre-Romantic poet, writing a crucial half-century after Pope, dramatizes that different perspective. Blake was a member of the lower middle class and poor his whole life. Unlike Pope, he didn't live in an elegant mansion with an elaborate garden of several acres but in a grimy working-class neighborhood in London. The Overcultural order Blake denounces in "London" is the kind that narrows people's lives just as the constricted slum streets squeeze against them physically:

> I wander through each charter'd street,
> Near where the charter'd Thames does flow,
> And mark in every face I meet
> Marks of weakness, marks of woe.
>
> In every cry of every Man,
> In every Infant's cry of fear,
> In every voice, in every ban,
> The mind-forg'd manacles I hear.

Blake hears and speaks for the miserable: chimney sweeps, soldiers, young prostitutes, and the urban oppressed in general. Blake creates a sound link between the incanted word "*char*tered" and another key word "*mark*." To be "chartered" is to have one's existence legally recognized by some ruling authority, and it is used ironically here to mean that all natural exuberance and liberty have been straitjacketed away from the Thames River and those who live alongside it in London's narrow slum streets. Blake's fervent wish is that the "mind-forged manacles" of social and economic exploitation be broken. Pope was a great designer and admirer of gardens. In Pope's real, suburban Thames-bank gardens, aristocrats and the very wealthy strolled, conversed, and flirted. When Blake writes about a garden it is a visionary place that combines Eden and the love-gardens of Medieval erotic poetry. But once again, it is blighted by the repressive orderings of the Overculture, in this case that of priests who prohibit the expression of playful intimacy and sexuality:

The Garden of Love

I went to the Garden of Love,
And saw what I never had seen:
A Chapel was built in the midst,
Where I used to play on the green.

And the gates of this Chapel were shut,
And "Thou shalt not" writ over the door;
So I turn'd to the Garden of Love,
That so many sweet flowers bore,

And I saw it was filled with graves,
And tomb-stones where flowers should be;
And Priests in black gowns were walking their rounds,
And binding with briars my joys and desires.

If "order" is a key value-term for Pope, then "liberty" is the
equivalent for Blake, and by liberty he means the vitalizing disorder
of social and political change. An ardent supporter of the French
and American revolutions, Blake embraces the trauma of change as
an opportunity to rebuild England entirely as the visionary city of
Jerusalem:

And did those feet in ancient time
Walk upon England's mountains green?
And was the holy Lamb of God
On England's pleasant pastures seen?

And did the Countenance Divine
Shine forth upon our clouded hills?
And was Jerusalem builded here
Among these dark Satanic Mills?

Bring me my Bow of burning gold:
Bring me my Arrows of desire:
Bring me my Spear: O clouds unfold!
Bring me my Chariot of fire.

I will not cease from Mental Fight,
nor shall my Sword sleep in my hand
till we have built Jerusalem
in England's green & pleasant Land.
(preface to "Milton")

Blake's Jesus might be the Lamb of God, but he's also the radical warrior who tossed the moneylenders out of the temple. Such a figure had both the power and desire to tear down the "dark Satanic Mills" whose wheels were grinding up souls as well as coal, whose looms were tearing apart the physical and emotional lives of workers even as they were weaving bolts of cloth.

Romanticism and the Personal Lyric

Certainly, there were other lyric poets who were less sanguine than Blake about the cataclysmic changes that were utterly altering their world. After all, the hopes and ideals of the French Revolution had quickly shifted into the relentless violence and guillotinings of the Terror. Still, if you were a poet, Romanticism was the new flag under which you were likely to muster and march toward the future. Inspired by Rousseau, the Romantics took lyric back from the Overculture. Returning it to its ancient and honorable identity as personal lyric, they used it according to its primordial function of ordering individual lives around emotionally charged experiences and restabilizing the self in a chaotic time.

It is in the context of the personal lyric and its subset, the transformative lyric, that certain figures emerge; poets who, coping with their own crises and traumas, seized the opportunity to create new selves and new meanings through the making of poems. These poets became poet-heroes by disclosing visionary possibilities that went far beyond their own private situations and revealed hopes and meanings that were broadly useful to others, both contemporaries and those of us who came after. They fulfilled Keats's dream of being "physician to all men." Of course, the term "all men" is hyperbolic and, to our postfeminist ears, restrictively sexist. It would be more accurate and thus more complimentary to say that these visionary poets were physicians to broad spectrums of the population who identified with their sense of trauma and confusion and their need for self-transformation.

Romanticism and its aftermath gave us hero after hero of spiritual renewal through the personal lyric. Their values and visions still have the power to sustain and inspire us, as we float on our rafts down the riotous currents and flood-swirls of that river formed when capitalism and technology flowed together and washed over the banks, inundating churches and government buildings, sweeping away the quiet villages, carrying all before it into a fluid, uncertain future.

CHAPTER TEN

Wordsworth and the Permanent Forms

More than anyone before him, William Wordsworth (1770–1850) brought poetry down out of the high-flown literary language that so subtly served the Overculture's class interests. The language in a poem, he said, should "consist of a selection of the real language spoken by men." With that single, simple idea, he brought poetry closer to the average person and connected it to the urgencies in people's lives. He insisted that a poet was neither a special, divinely inspired genius nor a spokesman for the Overculture and a propagandist for its values. Instead, the poet was simply "a man speaking to men," trying to communicate to them something urgent and using the compressed and lucid force of a poem to do so.

What was it that Wordsworth, in particular, felt an urgency about communicating? Without doubt, Wordsworth's affirmative message centered in the consoling and sustaining power of the natural world and how that power enters us deeply during childhood. Following Rousseau, Wordsworth in his early poems explored and celebrated the power of rural and wild landscapes to shape people morally, to help them become peaceable and contented individuals. This same natural world could also sustain them emotionally when they suffered.

Earlier, like many other young, idealistic men of his generation throughout Europe, Wordsworth had placed great faith in the political and economic transformations promised by the French Revolution with its Universal Declaration of the Rights of Man. But again, like many others, he was dismayed to witness what had seemed like

a liberal transformation of society slip toward the barbarous anar-
chy of the Reign of Terror and then revert to another version of
despotism under Napoleon. Wordsworth's political disillusionment
led him to search further back in his youth for a source of new values
and new ways of being. This led him to a celebration of childhood
exuberance growing up in a rural area, embodied especially in his
long, autobiographical poem, *The Prelude, or Growth of a Poet's Mind.*

Wordsworth's vision begins with childhood and is essentially an
idealized theory of how a healthy, moral adult consciousness could
develop out of a child's experience of the natural world and rural life.
Wordsworth believed that who we are as children largely determines
what kind of adult we will become. "The Child is Father of the
Man" is how he aphoristically puts it at the beginning of his "Ode:
Intimations of Immortality." The notion that our childhoods have
an important bearing on what kind of adult we become is, of course,
a commonplace of our contemporary psychological understanding,
but it wasn't always the case. Wordsworth's poetry was essential in
turning our Western attention to childhood and its complexities
and intensities. Wordsworth's vision of the child's psychological and
moral development centers in the idea of "sympathy"—the notion
that things respond emotionally to other things. In his view, humans
respond sympathetically to nature's influence and presence, which
is mostly benevolent. Thus, writing about his own infancy in *The
Prelude*, he claims the Derwent River he was born beside was as
actively involved in his upbringing as his human nurse. According
to Wordsworth, the Derwent

> loved
> to blend his murmurs with my nurse's song,
> And, from his alder shades and rocky falls,
> And from his fords and shallows, sent a voice
> That flowed along my dreams. . . .
> (Book 1, ll. 270–74)

Nature's sympathetic influence has the power to shape the emotional
and moral nature of the child, especially by calming him:

> For this, didst thou,
> O Derwent! winding among grassy holms
> Where I was looking on, a babe in arms,
> Make ceaseless music, that composed my thoughts
> To more than infant softness, giving me,
> Amid the fretful dwellings of mankind
> A foretaste, a dim earnest, of the calm
> That Nature breathes among the hills and groves. (ll. 274–81)

If we are tempted to think Wordsworth's vision is naively sentimental about nature, we should note that he thinks fear is as important as beauty in the proper development of consciousness: "Fair seed-time had my soul, and I grew up / Fostered alike by beauty and by fear" (ll. 301–2). Thus in a scene where the young Wordsworth (not yet ten) goes out at night to check whether his snares have caught birds, he yields to the temptation to steal a bird caught in someone else's snares and hallucinates something pursuing him:

> Ere I had told
> Ten birth-days . . . 'twas my joy,
> With store of springes [snares] o'er my shoulder hung
> To range the open heights where woodcocks run
> Along the smooth green turf. Through half the night,
> Scudding away from snare to snare, I plied
> That anxious visitation;—moon and stars
> Were shining o'er my head; I was alone,
> And seemed to be a trouble to the peace
> That dwelt among them. Sometimes it befel,
> In these night-wanderings, that a strong desire
> O'erpowered my better reason, and the bird
> Which was the captive of another's toil
> Became my prey; and when the deed was done
> I heard, among the solitary hills,
> Low breathings coming after me. (ll. 306–23)

The fear and terror of these "low breathings" are part of the shaping of the boy's conscience. The whole world of nature and the boy's mind and body are so interconnected through sympathy and feeling that the moral life emerges from the boy's constant contact with nature:

> To every natural form, rock, fruit or flower,
> Even the loose stones that cover the high-way,
> I gave a moral life; I saw them feel,
> Or linked them to some feeling: the great mass
> Lay bedded in a quickening soul, and all
> That I beheld respired with inward meaning.
> (Book 3, ll. 130–35)

These shapings and guidings of nature continue through adolescence and become a part of the adult's spiritual resources. One of Wordsworth's most famous opening lines presents an adult self seeking stability and consolation in the natural world: "I wandered lonely as a cloud." As the poem's speaker explores the landscape, he discovers thousands of daffodils waving in the wind by a lake. When he's "pensive" or "vacant" a long time later, he'll call up a vision of those flowers, and it will lessen his loneliness.

But let's pause here to consider some odd aspects of Wordsworth's idealized vision of childhood and how it affects the child's psychological and moral development. As I have noted already, in this dynamic of identity development, the child is his own father ("The Child is Father of the Man"), and Nature has a maternal function.

If Nature is mother and the child is his own father, then Wordsworth is describing an orphan. In his poetic version of how a child grows, the human parents are absent. This simple but mysterious situation can lead us backward into the facts of Wordsworth's childhood and toward the trauma that initiated his extraordinary and still compelling vision.

William Wordsworth was, indeed, an orphan at an early age. His mother died when he was eight. At this same time, he suffered a second powerful blow when his beloved sister Dorothy was sent away to live with relatives, so that he didn't see her again for nine years. When he was thirteen, his father also died, and the remaining three brothers and William were placed under the guardianship of two indifferent uncles. William and his siblings felt the loss of their mother powerfully:

> Early died
> My honoured Mother, she who was the heart
> And hinge of all our learnings and our loves:
> She left us destitute, and, as we might,
> Trooping together. (Book 5, ll. 256–60)

And William especially:

> I was left alone
> Seeking the visible world, nor knowing why.
> The props of my affections were removed,
> And yet the building stood, as if sustained
> By its own spirit! (Book 2, ll. 277–81)

He feels the primal nature of his loss, and yet he has mysteriously survived the loss. Still, survival alone is not enough. The world is full of numbed survivors. Wordsworth must transform his destitution and forlornness into something positive, something he can affirm and celebrate. And it is here that he takes the raw material of loss and desolation and from it creates a vision of sustaining nature. Here, the sympathetic intertwining of nature and self comes forward to rescue the traumatized child. It is not only that Nature can substitute for mother (even as the boy-child fathers himself), but that Nature is more stable and permanent. He can address her with a confidence he could not feel toward a mortal figure: "Knowing that Nature never did betray / The heart that loved her." After all, experience has taught Wordsworth that human parents can vanish suddenly into death and leave their children bereft. But Nature is *always there*—it is the world around us, ready to welcome us if we open ourselves to it:

> 'tis her [Nature's] privilege,
> Through all the years of this our life, to lead
> From joy to joy: for she can so inform
> The mind that is within us, so impress

With quietness and beauty, and so feed
With lofty thoughts, that neither evil tongues,
Rash judgements, nor the sneers of selfish men,
Nor greetings where no kindness is, nor all
The dreary intercourse of daily life,
Shall e'er prevail against us, or disturb
Our cheerful faith, that all which we behold
Is full of blessings.
("Lines Composed a Few Miles above Tintern Abbey," ll. 123–34)

Wordsworth's poems didn't "invent" nature, but they invented a relationship to nature. It is this eros of self and nature that has been a great gift to those who came after, a vision of something "deeply interfused" between the self and the world around it. Even today, we feel that a hike in the woods, or a pause to consider some vista or to observe closely some single flower, has the strength to ease our worries and lift from us the burden of misery or despair.

A SECOND MAJOR aspect of Wordsworth's vision has to do with childhood as a blessed and intense place. Wordsworth doesn't think he's idealizing the child he defines and defends. He sees him as flesh and blood: a vital rascal, not a perfect angel and (most of all) not a little adult. The child is someone who inhabits a world of passions and wildness and curiosity—of "play" that gradually becomes something calmer and deeper.

Of course, Wordsworth generalizes from his own experiences growing up in the rural landscape along the northwest coast of England and, especially, his time attending school in the Lake District. There, among wild hills, shepherds, and lakeside hamlets, he went to a private school and boarded with a simple village woman in her cottage. It was nothing fancy, and the schooling wasn't first-rate either. But that wasn't the center of his experience, wasn't what was valuable and essential. It was roving through the hills, trooping along the lake shore exploring with other boys, and also certain experiences alone in nature. In his lyric poems and in numerous episodic passages in *The Prelude*, Wordsworth describes his activities with loving accuracy and attention.

It may well be that Wordsworth paid such attention to his childhood and adolescent experiences partly because he had turned *away* from the human and social world after his parents' death and his sister's departure—that is, he withdrew into nature. But he transformed that withdrawal from the morbidity implied by the word "forlorn" into something far more positive and self-empowering found in the word "solitude." Thus, the young boy's aloneness became, in the adult poet's imaginings, a source of strength. And not only for himself but for countless other wounded selves who would read his poems. Wordsworth's writing about childhood in rural and wild settings can even inspire visions of freedom and spontaneity in people who grew up in urban or suburban environments.

Thus Wordsworth's contemporary and friend Samuel Coleridge, trapped as a youth in urban settings, was sustained by the visions of freedom he found in Wordsworth's early poems and hoped fervently to raise his own child differently and in a different environment:

> My babe so beautiful! it thrills my heart
> With tender gladness, thus to look at thee,
> And think that thou shalt learn far other lore
> And in far other scenes! For I was reared
> In the great city, pent 'mid cloisters dim,
> And saw nought lovely but the sky and stars.
> But *thou*, my babe! shalt wander like a breeze
> By lakes and sandy shores, beneath the crags
> Of ancient mountain, and beneath the clouds . . .
> (Coleridge, "Frost at Midnight")

These complementary aspects of Wordsworth's vision (that rural nature can form and sustain our emotional and moral growth, and that childhood is, at least potentially, a state of grace and freedom) are by no means all that his poetry is about, or all that he intended in his vision. Some of Wordsworth is dated and didn't survive past his century. Other notions are too quaintly expressed to move us now. But the project he entered on was successful, and these two aspects of his vision have continued to encourage anguished and questing individuals in our culture ever since. And today, Wordsworth also saves us less directly, through his heirs. Those nature poets who have emerged from his vision have created variations on it that bear the stamp of their own agony and its transformations: Gerard Manley Hopkins and Walt Whitman in the nineteenth century, Robert Frost in the twentieth, and, among more recent American poets, Theodore Roethke, Stanley Kunitz, James Wright, Mary Oliver, and Wendell Berry.

Wordsworth's imagination, struggling to transform his own traumatic plight and discover what could sustain and heal him, found sources of renewal that others could use also. His gift to us was a vision of eros-connections between self and nature, self and other selves. As he remarked in a poem to his friend and fellow-visionary Coleridge:

> Others will love what we have loved,
> And we shall teach them how.

CHAPTER ELEVEN

Keats and the Ardor
of the Pursuer

Born in 1795, Keats was among the younger generation of Romantic poets who grew up when Wordsworth's influence was dominant. He came from a lower-middle-class family (his father ran a livery stable), and he had no prospects of higher education. At the age of sixteen, he was apprenticed to an apothecary-surgeon and later studied medicine at Guy's and St. Thomas's hospitals in London. Our contemporary notion of a surgeon as a highly trained specialist is not appropriate to Keats's prospect. In his time, a surgeon was a medically trained person whose skills seldom went beyond setting broken bones and lancing boils. Nevertheless, Keats soon abandoned that modest career in favor of the truly unlikely prospect of becoming a poet. Like Wordsworth, Keats was an orphan. His father died when he was nine, his mother of tuberculosis when he was not quite fifteen. Nor were those the last of his intimate losses before he himself died of tuberculosis at the age of twenty-six. When Keats was twenty-three, his younger brother Tom died of tuberculosis in his arms. From childhood on, Keats was an extremely emotional and volatile person, and it's fair to say these losses gave a deeply melancholy cast to his preoccupations.

Young Keats was obsessed with becoming a poet. Never has anyone in the history of English poetry developed so quickly and produced great work so rapidly at such a young age. Almost all his great poems were written in a three-year span. What we know of Keats's inner life, we know from his fervent, eloquent, and entertaining letters. Keats's letters are remarkable for the insight they give us into his thinking about poetry and life. They also show us an anguished but vital mind in the process of figuring out how art (and especially poetry) can respond to some of the most disturbing and discouraging questions about life. Together, the letters form a kind of autobiography recording his extraordinary transformation from an ill-educated enthusiast to one of the English language's most enduring poets of passion. A great deal of his growth can be seen in his assimilation of lessons from his predecessors, especially Milton and Spenser, and always and above all, Shakespeare. But equally important were the psychological or existential transformations he accomplished through a fusing of ardor and imagination.

Testimony from his friends about Keats's personality centers on how genial he was, but also how moody and passionate. He could go from joy to despair with hardly a pause between. How was Keats to achieve any stability between his hyperawareness of suffering and death and his consciousness of his own volatile subjectivity? His letters tell us that such traumatic losses made him question whether there was anything of value or reliability in existence: "I scarcely remember counting upon any Happiness—I look not for it if it be not in the present hour—nothing startles me beyond the Moment. The setting Sun will always set me to rights—or if a Sparrow come before my Window I take part in its existence and pick about the Gravel" (Nov. 22, 1817).

This is not to be confused with the blatherings of someone exquisitely sensitive to beauty. We are hearing the voice of some-one who lives in a world of enormous instability and jeopardy but is determined to locate and seize, within that chaos, moments of experience that will "set him to rights." When he tells us he "becomes" the Sparrow picking at gravel on his window ledge, he is describing a resource he has developed to deal with his despair—letting go of his own embodied self and "becoming" something else, becoming the small bird hopping about.

Such a loss of self, a loss of embodied self-sense, is what a psychologist of trauma would call a fugue state. It happens when someone feels he or she is completely detached or emotionally and physically dissociated from their body. It is a common defense against the violence of trauma. A classic instance of a fugue state and the circumstances that give rise to it is that of a child being sexually abused. In order to defend against the overwhelming fear and suffering, the child's mind/imagination detaches and she feels she is floating above the bed near the ceiling or sitting in a corner of the room, watching someone hurt a doll or manipulate a puppet. Such a detachment takes place when the victim cannot bear the intensity of negative feelings and powerlessness. It works. It helps the self survive the agony. But a trauma victim may experience such fugue states later in life also, either when trauma is repeated or in other situations of high stress. These dissociative states are not chosen freely by the victim, especially when they recur in inappropriate circumstances.

But Keats transforms the instinctive and involuntary defensive nature of the fugue state and puts it in the service of a self "looking for happiness." In Keats's version, the self enters the fugue state at will and with conscious intent. Thus self-transcendence and sympathetic identification become techniques for restoring emotional equilibrium and gaining temporary release from the burden of despair and misery. But as Keats also points out in a letter written in the following month, such a skill helps Shakespeare create his vivid characters by "becoming" them. And such a chosen and willed fugue state is at the heart of one of his greatest poems, "Ode to a Nightingale."

The plot action of the nightingale ode is negligible, but the emotional and psychological territory it covers is considerable. As the poem opens, the poet hears the bird singing and is taken with how beautiful the song is, feels a sympathetic happiness as he listens. But the poet is aware that he is on the ground and the bird is up there, among the shadowy branches of a tree. It isn't just gravity that keeps Keats on the ground, but a sense of the heaviness and agony of the mortal human condition:

> Here, where men sit and hear each other groan;
> where palsy shakes a few, sad, last gray hairs,
>   Where youth grows pale, and spectre-thin, and dies;
>   Where but to think is to be full of sorrow
>   And leaden-eyed despairs . . . (ll. 24–28)

Keats considers two methods all cultures have employed for trans-
porting burdened selves up and out of their bodies: drugs and alcohol. He feels strange right away as he listens to the bird: "as if of
hemlock I had drunk, / or emptied some dull *opiate* to the drains."
He considers the use of alcohol to lift him up and out of his body in
ecstasy—wine might help him rise up toward the bird "charioted
by Bacchus and his pards [leopards]." Bacchus here is Dionysus, the
god of wine, whom the Greeks regarded as their greatest benefactor,
because his gift brought relief from woe. Both wine and opiates are
ways of inducing temporarily the beneficial release from a conscious
sense of being "trapped" in our own embodiment. But Keats proposes another technique of release:

> Away! away! for I will fly to thee,
>   Not charioted by Bacchus and his pards,
> But on the viewless wings of Poesy . . . .
> Already with thee! tender is the night.

Keats will fly there on the invisible wings of imagination rather than
through the use of drugs or alcohol. Seldom has a more urgent and
interesting notion been expressed in such unfortunate phrasing as
Keats's "viewless wings of Poesy." The phrase is flowery rhetoric
left over from the eighteenth century—the sort of artificial poetic
language Wordsworth struggled to free poetry from—but the notion itself is of utmost human significance and concerns the trained
human mind's ability to travel instantly to some imagined place and
experience that place with hallucinatory vividness.

Keats will, as the poem goes on to show, experience intense and
unusual sensations and thoughts in this altered state imagination
made possible. But, finally, such an ecstatic state cannot last. Keats's
poem describes what I would call a "parabola of transcendence."

What (or who) goes up, must come down. The disembodied self up there near the singing bird must crash back to earth again and re-inhabit its body with all the alienation and limitation that implies. It is worth noting that a word, the key word "forlorn," is the trigger that snaps Keats out of the ecstatic state of being "up there" with the bird ("thee") and plummets him back into his embodied self:

> Forlorn! the very word is like a bell
> To toll me back from thee to my sole self! (ll. 71–72)

He's then left with a question that haunts him in other poems also:

> Was it a vision, or a waking dream?
> Fled is that music:—Do I wake or sleep?

In other words, was it just a hallucinatory experience (waking dream) that offered a brief release from my suffering, or was it a glimpse of a higher reality (vision), which can be reached through intense emotion harnessed to imagination? The poem ends with the question—it asks but does not answer. In a letter, however, Keats does answer with an affirmation of feeling and imagination: "I am certain of nothing but of the holiness of the Heart's affections and the truth of Imagination—What the imagination seizes as Beauty must be truth—whether it existed before or not—for I have the same Idea of all our Passions as of Love they are all in their sublime, creative of essential Beauty" (Nov. 22, 1817).

KEATS WAS AN exuberant person, but he also had to continually struggle against a profound morbidity that made him feel there was no value in life. It is against the backdrop of this deep melancholy that another of Keats's "gifts" to us emerges: the notion that a person's passion for something is what creates meaning in their world. Here is the key passage from Keats's letter of March 13, 1818:

> So probably every mental pursuit takes its reality and worth from
> the *ardor of the pursuer*—being in itself a Nothing—Ethereal things

may at least be thus real, divided under three heads—Things real—things semireal—and no things. Things real—such as existences of Sun Moon & Stars and passages of Shakespeare—Things semireal such as Love, the Clouds etc which require *a greeting of the Spirit* to make them wholly exist—and Nothings which are made Great and dignified *by an ardent pursuit*. (my italics)

According to Keats's thinking, some things are real in and of themselves (sun, moon, stars, and certain passages of Shakespeare). Everything else is either semireal or a nothing. The semireal needs a "greeting of the spirit" to become wholly real, but a "no thing" can achieve greatness through the passion of the person who worships it or pursues it. Personal passion creates value, meaning, significance. If we care about something passionately, Keats tells us, then our passion will make that thing meaningful and important. And that elevated thing will, in turn, give meaning and purpose to our lives as we pursue it.

Keats is a great poet of love and desire, and, of course, in the realm of passionate love we see this "vision" functioning most obviously. When someone loves someone else, desires him or her passionately, then that love-object/person "becomes" beautiful, becomes "valuable" precisely in proportion to the desire and "ardor" the lover feels. When we love someone, he or she is beautiful to us. Their beauty isn't objective. In fact, it was our love that made them beautiful (in our eyes), gave them meaning (in our eyes). Keats's claim isn't just egotism, though it is strongly centered in the passionate emotional life of the individual desirer. It is a way that people create meanings: through the power of their desire. And these meanings sustain the desirer, sustain him or her in a world that might otherwise seem desolate and empty.

The passion that creates meaning needn't just be erotic, but it must be ardent. You must care with intensity in order to add value and meaning, add "reality" to things, says Keats.

Soul-Making

The first thing that strikes me on hearing a Misfortune
having befalled another is this "Well it cannot be
helped—he will have the pleasure of trying the resources
of his spirit."
November 22, 1817

Keats affirms radical subjectivity by claiming that passion
invests things with meaning and intensifies our own being. While
this affirmation of the power of passion is important, it doesn't
necessarily produce a stabilized self. Romeo is a passionate youth
and his passion invests Juliet with enormous significance, but only
the day before he had been, if we believe his early words, equally
infatuated with Rosalind and singing her praises. Is the lyric self
in Keats's world inherently unstable and subject to the whim of its
own passions? Yes and no. Keats also imagines a larger project called
"soul-making" by which the feeling self actively assimilates trauma
and grows deeper and more stable through such an activity.

Keats begins his vision of "soul-making" by criticizing the Christian idea of passive suffering. He rejects the image of life as a "vale
of tears" through which the pilgrim self must journey in order to
arrive, after death, in the divinely ordered landscape of heaven:

The common cognomen of this world among the misguided and
superstitious is "a vale of tears" from which we are to be redeemed by
a certain arbitrary interposition of God and taken to Heaven—What
a little circumscribed straightened notion! Call the world if you Please
"The vale of Soul-making." Then you will find out the use of the
world. . . . I say "*Soul making*. . . ." How then are Souls to be made?
How then are these sparks which are God to have identity given
them—so as ever to possess a bliss peculiar to each one's individual
existence? How, but by the medium of a world like this? (letter of
April 1819)

He goes on to compare the world to a school "instituted for the
purpose of teaching little children to read":

> I will call the *human heart* the *horn Book* [i.e., elementary text] used in that School—and I will call the *Child able to read, the Soul* made from that *School* and its *hornbook*. Do you not see how necessary a World of Pains and troubles is to school an Intelligence and make it a Soul? A place where the heart must feel and suffer in a thousand diverse ways! Not merely is the Heart a Hornbook, It is the Minds Bible, it is the Minds experience, it is the teat from which the Mind or intelligence sucks its identity. As various as the Lives of Men are—so various become their Souls, and thus does God make individual beings (into) Souls. . . . This appears to me a faint sketch of a system of Salvation which does not affront our reason and humanity.

According to Keats's vision of soul-making, what begins in all of us as a "spark" of Intelligence must be transformed through passionate emotional engagement (the Heart) into an Identity, a stable, individualized self. The vale of soul-making proposes not a passive self, but an active, transformative one. Here it is not simply a matter of creating value through the "ardor of the pursuer" but of self-creation: bringing into being an enduring identity through active, deeply felt encounters with difficulty and even trauma. It is a spiritual achievement as profound and basic as a child's learning to read.

KEATS LOVED TO make up parables in his letters—elaborate metaphors that allowed him to express complex ideas about the meaning of life in vivid, simple terms. In another letter, Keats unfolds a series of images to express what he sees as his purpose as a poet in a world of suffering and trauma. Probably borrowing his basic metaphor (a house with many rooms, or mansions) from the Gospels, where Jesus uses the image to describe heaven, Keats instead applies the image to the human mind:

> I will put down a simile of human life as far as I now perceive it; that is, to the point to which I say we both have arrived at—Well— I compare human life to a large Mansion of Many Apartments, two of which I can only describe, the doors of the rest being as yet shut upon me. The first we step into we call the infant or thoughtless

Chamber, in which we remain as long as we do not think—We
remain there a long while, and notwithstanding the doors of the
second Chamber remain wide open, showing a bright appearance,
we care not to hasten to it; but are at length imperceptibly impelled
by the awakening of this thinking principle within us—we no sooner
get into the second Chamber, which I shall call the Chamber of
Maiden-Thought [i.e., first thought], than we become intoxicated
with the light and atmosphere, we see nothing but pleasant wonders,
and think of delaying there for ever in delight: However among the
effects this breathing is father of is that tremendous one of sharpening
one's vision into the heart and nature of Man—of convincing one's
nerves that the world is full of Misery and Heartbreak, Pain, Sickness
and oppression—whereby this Chamber of Maiden Thought becomes
gradually darken'd and at the same time on all sides of it many doors
are set open—but all dark—all leading to dark passages—We see
not the balance of good and evil. We are in a Mist. *We* are now in
that state—We feel the "burden of the Mystery," To this Point was
Wordsworth come as far as I can conceive when he wrote "Tintern
Abbey" and it seems to me that his Genius is explorative of those
dark Passages. Now if we live, and go on thinking, we too shall
explore them. (May 3, 1818)

When we have passed from the initial chamber into the second
room, where we are at first stunned by the bliss and wonder of
the world, it's as if the very act of breathing (thinking?) leads us
to see "into the heart and nature of Man" and also become aware
that the world "is full of Misery and Heartbreak, Pain, Sickness and
oppression." In other words, this thinking leads to knowledge in
two directions: into human nature and into the surrounding world
of social relationships and physical suffering—that is, into inner and
outer disorder. This "breathing" or sharpened thinking darkens the
mysterious light in the room, and as the room darkens numerous
open doors leading to dark corridors are revealed.

Now, it is essential to step back from Keats's parable and realize it is
a model of the human mind and that the dark passages to be explored
are the mysteries of human thinking and feeling. Later in this same
letter, Keats declares Milton to be an inferior poet to Wordsworth

because "he did not think into the human heart, as Wordsworth has done." For Keats, both components of consciousness, heart and mind, are full of "dark passages."

If the "vale of soul-making" proposes a quest of active self-creation for all individuals, then "dark passages" may be especially suited to poets and artists, who must explore and penetrate the mysteries of consciousness: find out what the heart holds, what the mind knows. Not what is already known set to rhyme, but what is still unknown: a poetry of risk and exploration, of encountering new and unknown disorderings and ordering them into poems. It is a heroic project stated in homely terms.

It is also an appropriate project since the collapse of the Over-culture and the rise of Romanticism have made the mysteries and instabilities of human subjectivity an urgent concern. Keats is fully prepared to investigate the realms of dream, vision, and heightened emotion that will, a hundred years later, be seen as manifestations of the unconscious mind. No wonder Freud, though proud of his own explorations of the dark passages of the human mind, noted that everything he described poets had known and dramatized long before in their poems.

Keats takes a central power of lyric poetry—its ability to help individuals survive existential crises by ordering their disorder—and makes it into a life-structuring quest. The poet is not simply writing poem after poem in order to survive but is embarked on a project of inner exploration that will benefit others as well. When the poet "thinks into the human heart," he is adding to what we all know about ourselves.

Although a deep sense of life's suffering lies behind the image of Keats's "dark passages" and vale of soul-making, his response to that grim vision is to urge us to become active and creative, not passive. Keats urges us to have faith in imagination and its power to incarnate and consolidate meanings in the sensuous bodies of poems.

CHAPTER TWELVE

Whitman and the Habit of Dazzle

By my life-lumps! becoming already a creator,
Putting myself here and now to the ambushed womb
   of the shadows.
"Song of Myself," section 41

It might seem odd to include Walt Whitman (1819–
1892) among my hero-poets who have transformed trauma into
visions of human possibility, because Whitman is so insistently and
ecstatically affirmative. Where is the trauma in his work? Indeed, the
philosopher and psychologist William James muttered aloud skep-
tically that Whitman was almost pathologically "healthy-minded"
and optimistic. Can such an exuberant poet actually fit our scheme?

We need to remember that a poet's poems *are* his or her self-
creation; that the self we meet in the poems is often the newly
created self that has replaced the shattered and traumatized self of
lived experience. The Whitman we meet in the pages of *Leaves of
Grass* is "a man cohered out of tumult and chaos," even if that
new man is reticent about the tumult and trauma that engen-
dered him.

But what is that chaos from which the new self is born? What
trauma precedes the magnificent act of self-creation that is Whitman's poetry? That is one of the greatest mysteries of Whitman
scholarship and biography. Whitman himself loved to hint that
something major and transformative happened to him, but he never
told what it was.

It's not that we lack biographical information. We know Whitman was a Brooklyn native, the self-educated son of a failed, alcoholic carpenter. After years as a printer and writer, he became a newspaper editor for one and another newspaper in the New York area (and, briefly, in New Orleans). He wrote a terrible novel promoting the anti-alcohol movement and a few bad, derivative poems. And then, at the age of thirty-six, he published at his own expense the 1855 edition of *Leaves of Grass*, the most original and profound book of poems ever published by an American. No one had ever read anything like it. The poems didn't rhyme, nor were they structured with meter. They were sublime and sexy at the same time, elevated and vulgar, mystical and profane. Above all, they were ecstatic— filled with the visionary rapture of someone awed by the beauty of the natural world:

> I believe a leaf of grass is no less than the journey-work of the stars,
> And the pismire [ant] is equally perfect, and a grain of sand, and the
>   egg of the wren,
> And the tree-toad is the chef-d'oeuvre for the highest,
> And the running blackberry would adorn the parlors of heaven.
> ("Song of Myself," section 31)

The speaker of these poems, if poems they were, was amazed not just by nature but by the world of people around him, which he praised in evocative, swiftly moving lists:

> The pure contralto sings in the organ loft,
> The carpenter dresses his plank, the tongue of his foreplane whistles its
>   wild ascending lisp,
> The married and unmarried children ride home to their Thanksgiving
>   dinner,
> The pilot seizes the king-pin, he heaves down with a strong arm,
> The mate stands braced in the whale-boat, lance and harpoon are ready,
> The duck-shooter walks by silent and cautious stretches,
> The deacons are ordain'd with cross'd hands at the altar.
> ("Song of Myself," section 15)

In other poems, he frankly celebrated his own carnal being:

> Divine am I inside and out, and I make holy whatever I touch or am
> touch'd from,
> The scent of these arm-pits aroma finer than prayer,
> This head more than churches, bibles, and all the creeds.
> If I worship one thing more than another it shall be the spread of my
> own body, or any part of it,
> Translucent mould of me it shall be you!
> Shaded ledges and rests it shall be you!
> ("Song of Myself," section 24)

TO MAKE SENSE of Whitman's unusual talent, I'll work backward, first presenting some crucial principles of his vision and then speculating on what experiential trauma might have given rise to them.

I'll start by saying that Whitman's is a spiritual vision, but one that insists on manifesting itself physically. When Whitman first published *Leaves of Grass* in 1855, he knew that it was a spiritual document as well as a book of poems. He even went so far as to refer to it as a "new bible." Though such a claim might sound outrageous in a poet, Whitman was not alone in his ambition. William Blake, possibly Whitman's only equal in the realm of poetic revelations of transformative states, also thought of his work as having a central religious/spiritual agenda. In particular, Blake presented an "infernal Bible" in his great poem *The Marriage of Heaven and Hell*—a compilation of devilish wisdom to offset the "one-sided" angelic bible of conventional Christianity, which Blake felt lacked energy and passion. Neither Blake nor Whitman thought of themselves simply as poets, nor did Whitman think of *Leaves of Grass* as merely a collection of poems. After its first publication, he revised it again in 1856 and then six more times up until his death. Each revision added new poems and sections of poems to the book, but it was always the same book, always the same title. In a sense, *Leaves of Grass* was the testament of his spiritual revelation/intuition; it could be tinkered with and added to, but it was always the one and only central document.

To write a new bible in the face of a firmly established and dominant Christian bible, Whitman took over conventional spiritual terms and radically redefined them. He began with the terms "body" and "soul." Centuries of Christian theology had asserted that humans have a body and a soul. The body is material and carnal and rots after death; the soul is immaterial, spiritual, and immortal, and leaves the body at death to go to its reward in heaven or, alternatively, punishment in hell. In the conventional Christian scheme, the soul is the source of all good, the body the source of all evil and corrupt impulses. In "Song of Myself," "Starting from Paumanok," and other poems, Whitman entirely reimagines the nature and relationship of the terms "body" and "soul."

How does he do this? First he says soul and body ("the other I am") have equal claims on his attention:

> I believe in you my soul, the other I am must not abase itself to you,
> And you must not be abased to the other.
> ("Song of Myself," section 5)

But to say that body and soul are equal and equally deserving of respect, while radical and shocking in his time, is only the beginning of Whitman's transvaluative program. Whitman is determined to bring the soul into the body, incarnate it, and—finally, daringly— to absorb all spirituality into embodied being:

> Behold, the body includes and is the meaning, the main concern, and includes and is the soul;
> Whoever you are, how superb and how divine is your body, or any part of it!
> ("Starting from Paumanok," section 13)

> And I will make the poems of my body and of mortality,
> For I think I shall then supply myself with the poems of my soul and of immortality.
> ("Starting from Paumanok," section 6)

But even such a drastic rewriting of the Christian terms, body and soul, is not enough for Whitman. He wishes to transform the spiritual and social world even further with the praise-claims of his poem. Men and women are equal, he declares (a radical social claim in his day):

I am the poet of the woman the same as the man,
And I say it is as great to be a woman as to be a man.
("Song of Myself," section 21)

The man's body is sacred and the woman's body is sacred.
("I Sing the Body Electric")

In another crucial step toward his full vision, the equality of the sexes takes on the mystery of sexuality and desire:

Urge and urge and urge,
Always the procreant urge of the world.

Out of the dimness opposite equals [i.e., man and woman] advance,
    always substance and increase, always sex.
("Song of Myself," section 3)

Not only are sexuality and desire placed on center stage, but this sexual equality is pressed further as Whitman announces his intention to show that women as well as men are sexually dynamic and desiring creatures:

And I will show of male and female that either is but the equal of the
    other,
And sexual organs and acts! do you concentrate in me, for I am
    determin'd to tell you with courageous clear voice to prove you
    illustrious.
("Starting from Paumanok," section 12)

Whitman wishes to transform the spiritual values and principles by which we live. He wishes to include all in his vision: all ethnicities, both genders, all impulses and passions. All to him are "acceptable." He is a radical egalitarian, a radical democrat, but even deeper is his message of personal psychological liberation. He has arrived to announce the end of the shames, guilts, and inhibitions that haunt individuals:

> Undrape! you are not guilty to me, nor stale nor discarded,
> I see through the broadcloth and gingham whether or no,
> And am around, tenacious, acquisitive, tireless, and cannot be shaken
> away.
> ("Song of Myself," section 7)

Nakedness for Whitman is a spiritual condition, a sign of arriving at the innocent and instinctive state of animals, so different from that of humans, who have allowed themselves to become mentally and emotionally diminished:

> I think I could turn and live with animals, they are so placid and
> self-contain'd,
> I stand and look at them long and long.
>
> They do not sweat and whine about their condition,
> They do not lie awake in the dark and weep for their sins,
> They do not make me sick discussing their duty to God,
> Not one is dissatisfied, not one is demented with the mania of owning
> things,
> Not one kneels to another, nor to his kind that lived thousands of years
> ago,
> Not one is respectable or unhappy over the whole earth.
> ("Song of Myself," section 32)

Whitman wishes to speak affirmatively for others: for those too uneducated or too inarticulate or oppressed to express themselves and (this especially) for those too ashamed:

> Through me many long dumb voices,
> Voices of the interminable generations of prisoners and slaves,
> Voices of the diseas'd and despairing and of thieves and dwarfs,
> Voices of cycles of preparation and accretion,
> And of the threads that connect the stars, and of wombs and of the
> father-stuff,
> And of the rights of them that others are down upon,

Of the deform'd, trivial, flat, foolish, despised,
Fog in the air, beetles rolling balls of dung.

Through me forbidden voices,
Voices of sexes and lusts, voices veil'd and I remove the veil,
Voices indecent by me clarified and transfigur'd.

I do not press my fingers across my mouth,
I keep as delicate around the bowels as around the head and heart,
Copulation is no more rank to me than death is.

I believe in the flesh and the appetites.
Seeing, hearing, feeling, are miracles, and each part and tag of me is a
    miracle.

("Song of Myself," section 24)

In Whitman's view the individual self, *his* self, and the self of others are reciprocal mirrors. He celebrates himself and he celebrates others:

Having pried through the strata, analyzed to a hair, counsel'd with
    doctors and calculated close,
I find no sweeter fat than sticks to my own bones.

In all people I see myself, none more and not one a barleycorn less,
And the good or bad I say of myself I say of them.

("Song of Myself," section 20)

In the preface to his 1855 edition of *Leaves of Grass*, Whitman articulates the two most fundamental principles of his vision: pride and sympathy. They both begin inside the individual self, and their dialectical relationship gives form and dynamism to Whitman's world:

The greatest poet does not moralize or make applications of
morals . . . he knows the soul. The soul has that measureless pride
which consists in never acknowledging any lessons but its own. But
it has sympathy as measureless as its pride and the one balances the
other and neither can stretch too far while it stretches in company
with the other. The inmost secrets of art sleep with the twain. The

greatest poet has lain close betwixt both and they are vital in his style and thoughts.

Pride and sympathy are the two pillars of his "new bible." Pride centers the self in its project of physical self-celebration. Sympathy allows the poet, through an act of imagination, to enter into the life of others. Between them, they create a dynamic relationship in which the self alternates between self-delighted self-celebration and a loss of self in the agonies or daily lives of others. If he felt only pride, the poet (or any person) would be a monster of egotism. If he felt only sympathy, he might become utterly lost in other existences and paralyzed and confused. But the two together create a vision that reveals "the inmost secrets of art" and a possible ethical life based on imagination.

As he says in the very opening lines of "Song of Myself," Whitman accepts and celebrates himself and accepts and celebrates others also:

> I celebrate myself, and sing myself,
> And what I assume you shall assume,
> For every atom belonging to me as good belongs to you.

In this mystical brotherhood of "atoms," selves exist as individuals and yet all share something at a deeper level. This is a vision of benevolent inclusion. It calls for the self to periodically give up its identity and feel what other people feel. Whitman demonstrates this "sympathy" (today, we would call it empathy):

> I do not ask the wounded person how he feels, I myself become the wounded person,
> My hurts turn livid upon me as I lean on a cane and observe.
> ("Song of Myself," section 33)

Though sympathy is at the moral center of Whitman's world, he mentions it explicitly in only two crucial passages:

> Whoever walks a furlong without sympathy walks to his own funeral drest in his shroud.
> ("Song of Myself," section 48)

And:

> I am he attesting sympathy,
> (Shall I make my list of the things in the house and skip the house that
>   supports them?)

("Song of Myself," section 22)

In the first image, we have a terrifying vision of Thanatos: walking to your own funeral dressed in your shroud. Death-in-life. Utter, desolate isolation from all others and complete forlornness. In the second image, one thinks of the long lists of people and things Whitman celebrates in "Song of Myself." These extensive catalogs are "lists of things in the house" of the world, but *the house itself* is not only the material, physical world but also the *moral* world of sympathy. The "house" is inner as well as external to the self.

WHITMAN'S VISION HAS serious social and political dimensions, but my purpose here is to emphasize those aspects that have the most impact on individual readers. For me, such an emphasis centers in the sensuous delight that sometimes takes Whitman outside himself into rapturous wonder at a natural object or other person. At other times, this response of wonder and prideful joy is directed at his own physical being.

But what is the origin of Whitman's remarkable poetic vision that wishes to include and celebrate us all, with all our flaws and failures? And how could such a healing vision be imagined as born out of trauma? As I said at the beginning of this section, Whitman himself is surprisingly reticent about details of his life, and especially about how his vision came into being. I will speculate, though my speculations are well grounded in what scholars and biographers have nosed out about our genius. Quite simply, Whitman was gay. Gay in a time and place when it was far less safe to be homosexual than it is now, when it was both illegal and dangerous to overtly profess such a sexual orientation. We have no direct, first-hand testimony of Whitman's homosexual orientation, nor would Whitman ever have acknowledged it, even to his closest friends and admirers. But sufficient evidence is there in poems and journal entries, especially those related to a decades-long crush on a Washington streetcar conductor named Peter Doyle. It is doubtful that Whitman was comfortable with his own sexual orientation; certainly the culture surrounding him would have been outraged at it. Can being a closeted gay constitute a trauma? Ample testimony from our own, more tolerant time indicates that this is so, especially among adolescents coming into their sexuality who discover that their inclinations and attractions are still regarded with enormous and often violent prejudice.

What I want to claim about Whitman is simply this: that to be gay in an intolerant, heterosexual world is to be an outsider, to be someone at the very fringes of the culture. Someone who personally feels the destructive force of guilt and shame. Whitman's homosexuality was hidden and had to be, nor could his most affectionate and passionate impulses be openly expressed. If Whitman experienced his society's hostility toward his amorous impulses as an alienating trauma, he would not be the first or last such person. But this, of course, is Whitman's transformative genius: to be one of the ultimate outsiders in his actual life and yet to create a persona in his poetic life, a "Walt Whitman" who is the ultimate insider. The Walt Whitman who says "I" throughout *Leaves of Grass* is someone whose "pride" overcomes shame and censure and whose "sympathy" allows him to enter into other people's lives and beings, especially their secret wishes. Often these secret wishes are full of longing for affection and intimacy, as in this passage, where he enters the mind of a young widow as she fantasizes about young men:

Twenty-eight young men bathe by the shore,
Twenty-eight young men and all so friendly;
Twenty-eight years of womanly life and all so lonesome.

She owns the fine house by the rise of the bank,
She hides handsome and richly drest aft the blinds of the window.

Which of the young men does she like the best?
Ah the homeliest of them is beautiful to her.

Where are you off to, lady? for I see you,
You splash in the water there, yet stay stock still in your room.

Dancing and laughing along the beach came the twenty-ninth bather,
The rest did not see her, but she saw them and loved them.

The beards of the young men glisten'd with wet, it ran from their long
  hair,
Little streams pass'd all over their bodies.

An unseen hand also pass'd over their bodies,
It descended tremblingly from their temples and ribs.

The young men float on their backs, their white bellies bulge to the
  sun, they do not ask who seizes fast to them,
They do not know who puffs with pendant and bending arch,
They do not think whom they souse with spray.
("Song of Myself," section 11)

We will never know whether or how intensely Whitman might have felt guilt, shame, and fear over his sexual orientation, but we do know that the vision of himself and his actions in his poems is very much the opposite of guilty and excluded. Whitman's poems are extraordinarily uninhibited. His "dream" is to be at the very center of his culture as the chief celebratory poet of American exuberance and democracy. He says as much in the final sentence of his preface to *Leaves of Grass*: "The proof of a poet is that his country absorbs him as affectionately as he has absorbed it." In reality, during his lifetime Whitman and his poetry were not absorbed affectionately and passionately by the American public. He was mostly ignored, occasionally reviled, and only rarely recognized as the genius he was. But what happened to Whitman the man is not the issue. Whitman the poet "translated" himself into language, created a new self to inhabit and preside over those extraordinary poems with grandeur and humane affection: "Walt Whitman, a kosmos, of Manhattan the son, / Turbulent, fleshy, sensual, eating, drinking and breeding" ("Song of Myself," section 24). And this new self is not inhibited and aloof, as Whitman the man often was. This new self we meet in the poems is the proud propounder of a vision of freely expressive selves, selves liberated not just from social prejudice and inhibition but from the far more powerful, inner bonds of shame, guilt, and fear. Recreating himself as the bold protagonist of compelling poems, Whitman prods us to take risks, become larger and more awake than we ordinarily are, more alert to the wonder of life and of our own being:

> Long enough have you dream'd contemptible dreams,
> Now I wash the gum from your eyes,
> You must habit yourself to the dazzle of the light and of every moment
> of your life.
>
> Long have you timidly waded holding a plank by the shore,
> Now I will you to be a bold swimmer,
> To jump off in the midst of the sea, rise again, nod to me, shout, and
> laughingly dash with your hair.
> ("Song of Myself," section 46)

CHAPTER THIRTEEN

Dickinson and the Brain's Haunted Corridors

I suppose there are depths in every Consciousness,
from which we cannot rescue ourselves—to which
none can go with us.
Dickinson to Mrs. J. G. Holland, June 1878

Emily Dickinson (1830–1886) could well be the ultimate poet of the personal lyric. No lyric poet has been her equal
for the intensity and variety of subjective states dramatized. She
has written great poems of grief, longing, wonder, loneliness, fear,
love, madness, joy, anger, ecstasy, solitude, despair, desire. She has
written wonderfully about the great mysteries of time and death,
and those imaginings that seem to cancel time and death: eternity
and immortality.

It would be possible to write an eight hundred–page biography
of Emily Dickinson (such a book has been written). But if that
biography confined itself to her activities in the world, it would
be appallingly repetitious and boring. In her sixty years of life, she
seldom left her small Massachusetts village of Amherst, and even
within the narrow compass of Amherst she had a tendency to stay
in her family's house. What's more, she preferred her own bedroom
to any other area of the house and would often retire there when
visitors arrived. Or she might lower a basket of gingerbread on a rope
from her bedroom window to an assembled group of neighborhood
children. Was she a timid and batty lady? A small town eccentric
who, after a certain point, dressed almost entirely in white? Yes. And

yes, the physical excursions she took were few and uninteresting, but her imaginative journeys were incessant, and the inner realm she inhabited was vast. She had one of the greatest imaginations of American poetry—the equal of Whitman's, though very different in tone. And she was one of the most adventurous and courageous minds of her time (and ours). She was what William Blake might call a "Mental Traveller," and her excursions constituted the most elaborate exploration ever of Keats's "dark passages" of consciousness.

Much as I admire Keats's image of the shadowy corridors of consciousness, it fails to do justice to the boldness and wildness of Emily Dickinson's exploring. We need the sort of rugged, American image Whitman would urge, something equal to the originality and primitive power of Dickinson's venture. Something like those huge cave systems that writhe and dive for hundreds of miles beneath the American soil: Mammoth in Kentucky or Carlsbad Caverns in New Mexico. I'm thinking less of the huge, operatic rooms hung with stalactites than the narrow windings that might end in a wall or a cliff or a small pool where tiny, blind fish swim. And Emily Dickinson, our Recluse of the White Dress, crawls there in her other, chthonic incarnation as America's Greatest Cave Explorer. While Emily Dickinson the proper Amherst damsel strolls about town and countryside observing flowers and sunsets with her dog Carlo, Emily Dickinson the intrepid Poet is deep underground, with her lantern helmet of intense rhythms and startling metaphors probing the dark, mapping states of consciousness no one else has had the courage or skill to articulate.

I say a cave system and I mean the human brain:

One need not be a Chamber – to be Haunted –
One need not be a House –
The Brain has Corridors – surpassing
Material Place –

Far safer, of a Midnight Meeting
External Ghost
Than its interior Confronting –
That Cooler Host.

Far safer, through an Abbey gallop,
The Stones a'chase –
Than Unarmed, one's a'self encounter –
In lonesome Place –

Ourself behind ourself, concealed –
Should startle most – (J. 670)

We know she wrote at least 1,775 lyric poems—a staggering number—because she preserved most of them in her spidery handwriting on small, hand-sewn packets she kept in a trunk. How to explain those 1,775 poems? She wrote more great poems than any other American poet before or since. And only five of them were published in her lifetime. Even those five were recast, repunctuated, printed without her permission. I know—she sent her poems to friends, enclosed copies of them in letters or in baskets of baked goods sent to neighbors, and so on. But the truth remains that almost no one around her could appreciate the audacity and originality of her work. To say that her genius was recognized and understood is simply not accurate. Her solitude was impenetrable. It was the solitude of someone who hears, inside her, an utterly distinct music, who endures and bodies forth utterly distinct and bold imaginings. It's as if she played an invisible harp in her room—a harp only she could see or hear. And each string was a different poem, a different lyric organized around a distinct, intense emotion. Each string was a poem and also a tightrope on which Emily Dickinson walked out and balanced over the Abyss. No safety net. Only the music in her ears, to which she danced, alone there on the wire.

IF LYRIC POETRY thrives on its intensity (as Keats claimed), then that intensity is often achieved through compression. Many of Dickinson's poems are imagistically and syntactically dense and hard to understand, and they move and shift their images with a kind of lightning rapidity that takes getting used to. I've been reading Dickinson's poems for years: I still feel that in the best of her poems there are always lines or images or turns of thought that I can't follow, and yet this in no way diminishes my sense that I have absorbed the energy and significance of the poem. For me, as a reader, the most important thing is to ignore her eccentric punctuation and read her poems *aloud*, listening for their *tone of voice*. Once I can hear the human voice of her emotion behind a particular poem, I feel as if I am inside the poem and its mystery or message is revealed to me. And once you hear her voice, it can be as direct and urgent as anything anyone ever said:

> I cannot live with You –
> It would be Life –
> And Life is over there –
> Behind the Shelf. (J. 640)

She continues with a metaphor of the frustrated lovers being locked up in a cupboard like broken or old-fashioned china cups; except that it is a sexton, a gravedigger, who locks up the cupboard, and on the poem goes to even more strange yet lucid imaginings.

Or:

> I measure every Grief I meet
> With narrow, probing, Eyes –
> I wonder if It weighs like Mine –
> Or has an Easier size.
>
> I wonder if They bore it long –
> Or did it just begin –
> I could not tell the Date of Mine –
> It feels so old a pain –
>
> I wonder if it hurts to live –
> And if They have to try –
> And whether – could They choose between –
> It would not be – to die. (J. 561)

WHAT WAS HER trauma? What hurt her into song? Though Emily Dickinson wrote thousands of letters to her friends and acquaintances, she had almost no one with whom she could discuss poetry writing. The one major exception was T. W. Higginson, a journalist and editor to whom she sent some poems in April 1862 and with whom she corresponded for years. In response to his first letter to her, inquiring how long she had been writing, she says the following:

> You asked how old I was? I made no verse—but one or two—until this winter—Sir— [In fact, she has written over two hundred by the time of this letter.]
>
> I had a terror—since September—I could tell to none—and so I sing, as the Boy does by the Burying Ground—because I am afraid— . . . When a little Girl, I had a friend, who taught me Immortality— but venturing too near, himself—he never returned. (April 25, 1862)

So, we know that a loss or losses amounting to "terror" are one motive she claims for writing. We learn about her sense of isolation and how she has turned to nature for consolation: "You ask of my Companions Hills—Sir—and the Sundown—and a Dog—large as myself, that my Father bought me—They are better than Beings— because they know—but do not tell—and the noise in the Pool, at Noon—excels my Piano."

We learn of her family, with whom she will spend her whole life, although she differs from them, especially in matters of religion: "I have a Brother and Sister—My Mother does not care for thought— and Father, too busy with his Briefs—to notice what we do [her father was a lawyer]—He buys me many Books—but begs me not to read them—because he fears they joggle the Mind. They are religious—except me—and address an Eclipse, every morning— whom they call their 'Father.' "

Her father might have feared books would destabilize Emily Dickinson, but it might be closer to the truth to note that she was so sensitive to her emotional states that, in a sense, anything was capable of joggling her mind: "When far afterward—a sudden light on Orchards, or a new fashion in the wind troubled my attention— I felt a palsy, here—the Verses just relieve—" (letter to Higginson, June 7, 1862). That is, her consciousness, her "attention" could be troubled and disordered by a sensation in nature or by her own emotional states—by outer or inner disorder, by joy and wonder (mostly in nature) as much as by terror, pain, despair, and grief (her inner weather). And when these "palsies" struck, she turned to the writing of poems to regain her balance.

When Higginson, responding to some poems she sent him, urges her to write a more regular meter, she responds with some more poems and some pertinent remarks:

> Are these more orderly? I thank you for the Truth—
> I had no Monarch in my life, and cannot rule myself; and when I try to organize—my little Force explodes—and leaves me bare and charred—
> I think you called me "Wayward." Will you help me improve?
> (letter of August 1862)

What can we "trust" in Dickinson's letters to Higginson? She is complex: she needs the sophisticated literary response and encouragement she gets from Higginson, but she also knows her own genius and originality, or at the very least she is committed to that originality and does not alter her poems to fit his criticism (though she makes a great show of gratitude in her letters to him). I think we can trust this: her image of being unable to "rule" herself; her sense that when she tries to "organize" and order her language and her emotions, she "explodes." This image isn't of someone who cannot write ordered poems—we see that she writes them masterfully and incessantly. Instead, it is testimony from someone who realizes that she is unstable, who knows that her volatile consciousness can blow up in her face, leaving her "bare and charred." And it is precisely this volatility that she incorporates into her poems in order to triumph over it and, in the process, creates the complex and multifaceted self we know as the Emily Dickinson of the poems.

HOW STRANGE TO BE Emily Dickinson. She is so much smarter and livelier than anyone around her—an inevitable conclusion for anyone who has experienced the delight of reading her letters. And yet, she is a woman. What can she do with her intelligence and imagination? She can't become a lawyer or doctor or professor. She can't go into business. All that her small-town New England world held out to her as possibilities were marriage and motherhood or spinsterhood. No wonder she thought she would burst. No wonder her poems explode.

With Emily Dickinson more than with any of my other heroes of imagination, I am concerned that by trying to pinpoint what specific trauma assailed her, I may be on the wrong track. Ultimately, it's pointless to attempt to locate the specific traumas that initiated the desolation and radical freedom that gave rise to the self-creation of her poems. All we could hope to do is guess. The worst situation of all would be the error of psychoanalytic criticism: to think that by locating and labeling the poet's trauma, we had found out his or her secrets. To think that way would be to look down the wrong end of the telescope at diminishment.

We need to go in the opposite direction: recognizing that the poet's trauma initiates the struggle of transformation that leads to the richly proliferating and glorious incarnations of the poems.

We can't know what hurt Emily Dickinson so, but we do know that something hurt her with enormous force, again and again:

> It struck me – every Day –
> The Lightning was as new
> As if the Cloud that instant slit
> And let the Fire through –
>
> It burned me – in the Night –
> It Blistered to My Dream –
> It sickened fresh upon my sight –
> With every Morn that came –
>
> I thought that Storm – was brief –
> The Maddest – quickest by –
> But Nature lost the Date of This –
> And left it in the Sky – (J. 362)

And we know that she responded bravely, that she "love(d) to buffet the sea!" She meant, of course, an *inner* sea: the sea of subjectivity, of the rise and fall, the ebb and flow and wild, wave-torn storms of the emotional life. Such storms, turned into words, might take the form of incantatory raptures on an imagined, intimate ecstasy:

> Wild Nights – Wild Nights!
> Were I with thee
> Wild Nights would be
> Our Luxury!
>
> Futile – the Winds –
> To a Heart in port –
> Done with the Compass –
> Done with the Chart!
>
> Rowing in Eden –
> Ah, the Sea!
> Might I but moor – Tonight –
> In Thee! (J. 249)

Or they might articulate despair and fear of madness:

> I felt a Funeral, in my Brain,
> And Mourners to and fro
> Kept treading – treading – till it seemed
> That Sense was breaking through –
>
> And when they all were seated,
> A Service, like a Drum –
> Kept beating – beating – till I thought
> My Mind was going numb –
>
> And then I heard them lift a Box
> And creak across my Soul
> With those same Boots of Lead, again,
> Then Space – began to toll,
>
> As all the Heavens were a Bell,
> And Being, but an Ear,
> And I, and Silence, some strange Race
> Wrecked, solitary, here –

And then a Plank in Reason, broke,
And I dropped down, and down –
And hit a World, at every plunge,
And Finished knowing – then – (J. 280)

Dickinson can hymn desolation and agony:

The Heart asks Pleasure – first –
And then – Excuse from Pain –
And then – those little Anodynes
That deaden suffering –

And then – to go to sleep –
And then – if it should be
The will of its Inquisitor
The privilege to die – (J. 536)

And just as fervently, the defiant free will of creativity exemplified
by the writing of poems:

They shut me up in Prose –
As when a little Girl
They put me in the Closet –
Because they like me "still" –

Still! Could themself have peeped –
And seen my Brain – go round –
They might as wise have lodged a Bird
For Treason – in the Pound –

Himself has but to will
And easy as a Star
Abolish his Captivity –
And laugh – No more have I – (J. 613)

She can articulate a sense of cryptic wonder:

I am afraid to own a Body –
I am afraid to own a Soul –
Profound – precarious Property – (J. 1090)

Or brood on the loss of religious faith:

> Those – dying then,
> Knew where they went –
> They went to God's Right Hand –
> That Hand is amputated now
> And God cannot be found – (J. 1551)

Or the mystical humbling of the human heart:

> Not with a Club, the Heart is broken
> Nor with a Stone –
> A Whip so small you could not see it
> I've known
>
> To lash the Magic Creature . . . (J. 1304)

WITH EMILY DICKINSON, it might seem as if we were talking about the poetry of survival—a restabilizing of self through poetic ordering. But subjectivity is so rampant and intense for Dickinson that the truest thing we might risk saying is that subjectivity *itself* could be said to constitute her trauma. Her emotional life was so excruciatingly volatile and her solitude so deep that simple conscious existence represented a potential shattering of self. And she responds to this curious threat with an equally powerful ordering self, a self created in and through the poems. When we think of the transformative lyric as a project in self-creation, it is worth noting that "I" is Emily's favorite opening word, beginning a full 142 of her poems (only "the" happens more frequently). Who knows the secret nature of the thin lady in white who sometimes opened the door at her father's house when the neighbors came calling? Much fruitless speculation has been expended on her thwarted romantic life—as if identifying this or that acquaintance as the love of her life might illuminate something.

Her true lovers were the three strange angels of Lawrence's poem, and when they knocked, she flung wide the door and embraced them. She became Our Lady of the Strange Angels, the Amherst Virgin immaculately conceiving and bringing forth poem after astonishing poem. She took each emotion, each mental state on its own terms and wrestled it into the small space her poems take up. And she challenges us to be her equal in courage:

Dare you see a Soul *at the White Heat*? (J. 365)

CHAPTER FOURTEEN

Wilfred Owen and the Horrors of War

In Wilfred Owen's time, during the First World War, they called it "shell shock." In the Second World War, it would be called "battle fatigue." It was only in the aftermath of the Vietnam War that the term "post-traumatic stress disorder" became established as a way to speak of the tens of thousands of Vietnam veterans whose minds and lives were permanently altered by their exposure to the violence of combat.

According to Judith Herman, the symptoms of post-traumatic stress disorder fall into three main categories—hyperarousal, intrusion, and constriction: "Hyperarousal reflects the persistent expectation of danger; intrusion reflects the indelible imprint of the traumatic moment; constriction reflects the numbing response of surrender" (*Trauma and Recovery* 35). What we know now is that the brain's chemistry and neural pathways are permanently altered by trauma, particularly by the intense powerlessness and terror associated with prolonged combat. Here is Owen's description of the incident that precipitated his shell shock:

> Never before has the Battalion encountered such intense shelling
> as rained on us as we advanced in the open [thirty men died in this
> barrage]. The Colonel sent round this message the next day: "I was
> filled with admiration at the conduct of the Battalion under the heavy
> shellfire. . . . The leadership of officers was excellent, and the conduct
> of the men beyond praise." The reward we got for all this was to
> remain in the Line [i.e., the battle line] for 12 days. For twelve days I
> did not wash my face, nor take off my boots, nor sleep a deep sleep.

> For twelve days we lay in holes, where at any moment a shell might put us out. I think the worst incident was one wet night when we lay up against a railway embankment. A big shell lit on the top of the bank, just 2 yards from my head. Before I awoke, I was blown in the air right away from the bank! I passed most of the following days in a railway Cutting, in a hole just big enough to lie in, and covered with corrugated iron. My brother officer of B Coy, 2/Lt Gaukroger, lay opposite in a similar hole. But he was covered with earth, and no relief will ever relieve him, nor will his Rest be a 9 days-Rest. (*Selected Letters* 238)

The editor of Owen's selected letters pinpoints the moment of being blown into the air as the precise cause of his shell shock, but we might just as plausibly point to the horrifying experience of twelve straight days of helplessness hunkered down under bombardment with the realization that at any moment you could be killed.

A person suffering from post-traumatic stress disorder might be unable to relax or feel safe in any situation (hyperarousal). They might suffer hallucinatory re-experiencing of the trauma (what we call "flashbacks") or other eruptions and interruptions of their normal life by vivid mental representations of the event, such as those Owen describes in "Mental Cases":

> Always they must see these things and hear them,
> Batter of guns and shatter of flying muscles,
> Carnage incomparable, and human squander
> Rucked too thick for these men's extrication.
>
> Therefore still their eyeballs shrink tormented
> Back into their brains, because on their sense
> Sunlight seems a blood-smear; night comes blood-black;
> Dawn breaks open like a wound that bleeds afresh. (ll. 15–22)

The victim might also shut down entirely into a numbed person unable to feel or respond emotionally to things or people.

WILFRED OWEN WAS a young Englishman of twenty-two when he joined the English Army in October of 1915. A little over a year later, he was in France moving toward the front lines. After four months of battle, he was sent home with shell shock. Four months later, he was judged recovered and returned to light military duty. After another seven months, he was considered fit for active duty and soon returned to France and the front lines. He was killed in action, at the age of twenty-five, only a week before the armistice that ended the war.

World War I was not like any war that preceded it. Though the armies of both sides were ready to fight, neither was prepared for the strange and massive savagery of it. It was not a war of decisive battles and breakthroughs but of fixed lines of trenches, hundreds of miles long. A war fought with murderous new products of technology: tanks, machine guns, poison gas, and huge artillery pieces that lobbed shells fifteen miles. A war that discovered No Man's Land, that space between the two trench lines strung with row on row of barbed wire, where bodies rotted for weeks and men disappeared in the bottomless mud churned up by artillery barrages. Here is Owen's description of this ghastly landscape in one of his first letters from the front: "It is pock-marked like a body of foulest disease and its odor is the breath of cancer. . . . No Man's Land under snow is like the face of the moon chaotic, crater-ridden, uninhabitable, awful, the abode of madness" (Jan. 19, 1917).

Nor was anyone prepared for the scale of casualties. The Allied death toll for the four years of the war was 5.1 million, with another 12.8 million wounded. The Central Powers lost 3.5 million in military deaths, with another 8.4 million wounded. Perhaps by sketching briefly a single example of this mass slaughter, we can at least bring its enormity into some focus. The Battle of the Somme took place in June 1916, when two long years of trench warfare should have made everyone aware that a decisive breakthrough of the heavily entrenched enemy lines was not possible for either side. The plan was a French-English attack along a twenty-five-mile front to be preceded by a seven-day barrage. The Allies launched over a million and a half artillery shells, but the Germans were hidden in reinforced bunkers forty feet deep in the ground. When the shelling ceased, the Germans emerged and started firing machine guns at the advancing waves of Allied foot soldiers. On that first day, the British lost 55,450 men, including 19,240 dead. They gained a mere thousand yards of territory. The battle continued until November 19. When it was over, the Allies had advanced only seven miles at the cost of 200,000 French casualties, 415,690 British, and 434,500 Germans. It was the bloodiest battle in history, and it accomplished nothing except to rearrange the trench lines.

But what does this have to do with poetry? The personal lyric does not deal with statistics; it centers in individual experience. What the personal lyric does and can do is give the individual human response to an experience of this appalling magnitude. But several things have to be remembered. In Owen's time, there was no precedent for these horrors of experience. Nor had poetry ever tried to deal with such visceral grimness, except possibly in Homer's *Iliad*, which is filled with grisly descriptions of battles and woundings. But the *Iliad*, while true to the visceral suffering of bodies in combat, was also a central pillar of the Greek Overculture. As an epic, it proffered "immortality" to the fiercest male warriors (heroes). The epic tradition promised these warriors that their deeds and names would be remembered long after their deaths, something literally inconceivable in Owen's time. Owen wrote of war in a lyric mode: "My subject is War, and the pity of War. The Poetry is in the pity." And: "All a poet can do today is warn."

OWEN WAS A very young poet. Most of his pre-war poems and many written during the war itself were generalized and sentimental. Like many another beginning poet, Owen was so intoxicated with the idea of poetry and so eager to write something that sounded like a poem that he could not resist filling his poems with received sentiments and phrases derived from the poets he worshipped (especially Keats). Pursuing what "sounds like poetry," such young poets often end up excluding from their poems the chaos around them and inside them. In short, Owen, like many apprentice poets, was armored against experience. Perhaps only the horrors of trench warfare, lurching marches across No Man's Land, and ceaseless artillery barrages could have broken down Owen's mental barriers and created an opening through which Lawrence's strange angels could enter.

But enter they did. Fierce as the Greek Furies who pursued Orestes. And they opened their rucksacks and dumped on the floor all those odd, terrifying objects that Owen had come to know and would now incorporate into his poems: gas masks, tanks, hand grenades, machine guns, barbed wire, flamethrowers, snipers, mud and guts, and rotting bodies in shell holes—all those objects English poetry had never before acknowledged. (I don't want to overstate Owen's originality. He was strongly urged in the direction of acknowledging his traumatic experience by Sigfried Sassoon, a fellow soldier and poet he met at Craiglockhart Hospital, where both were being treated for shell shock and where Sassoon was being detained because he had begun to agitate for pacifism.)

What happened was that the trauma of unrelenting combat helped Owen overcome his own denial of the reality of his experience. Of course, Owen's personal denial was shared by almost the entire English public and encouraged by the army's propaganda machine. Patriotism and high, abstract sentiments about sacrifice were what people wanted to hear and what the government wished to encourage in poetry about the war. The truth of the soldiers' suffering and the horrific scale of the casualties was not what the culture was prepared to acknowledge. So Owen had to triumph over his own personal denial and that of his surrounding culture in order to write such experience-filled poems as "Dulce et Decorum Est" (1918), which takes its title from the opening lines of an ode by the Roman poet Horace—"Sweet and fitting it is to die for one's country"—and gives them a savagely ironic twist:

> Bent double, like old beggars under sacks,
> Knock-kneed, coughing like hags, we cursed through sludge,
> Till on the haunting flares we turned our backs
> And toward our distant rest began to trudge.
> Men marched asleep. Many had lost their boots

But limped on, blood-shod. All went lame; all blind;
Drunk with fatigue; deaf even to the hoots
Of tired, outstripped Five-Nines that dropped behind.

Gas! GAS! Quick, boys!—An ecstasy of fumbling,
Fitting the clumsy helmets just in time;
But someone still was yelling out and stumbling
And flound'ring like a man in fire or lime . . .
Dim, through the misty panes and thick green light,
As under a green sea, I saw him drowning.

In all my dreams, before my helpless sight,
He plunges at me, guttering, choking, drowning.

If in some smothering dreams you too could pace
Behind the wagon that we flung him in,
And watch the white eyes writhing in his face,
His hanging face, like a devil's sick of sin;
If you could hear, at every jolt, the blood
Come gargling from the froth-corrupted lungs,
Obscene as cancer, bitter as the cud
Of vile, incurable sores on innocent tongues,—
My friend, you would not tell with such high zest
To children ardent for some desperate glory,
The old Lie: Dulce et decorum est
Pro patria mori.

Owen's transformation takes place in two stages. In the first, a callow youth arrives at the war front and is at first exhilarated by what he finds there, but finally, under the stress of incessant bombardment, is destroyed emotionally and left with what they call shell shock. This first transformation is entirely negative and destructive of the self, of course. If Owen remained in this state, as hundreds of thousands of World War I veterans did, we would never have heard of him or read his poems. This shattering of trauma usually leads to that silence noted by the essayist Walter Benjamin in his 1923 essay "The Storyteller":

Was it not noticeable at the end of the war that men returned from the battlefield grown silent—not richer, but poorer in communicable experience? And there was nothing remarkable about that. . . . A generation that had gone to school on a horse-drawn streetcar now stood under the open sky in a countryside in which nothing remained unchanged but the clouds, and beneath these clouds, in a field of force of destructive torrents and explosions, was the tiny, fragile human body. (*Illuminations* 84)

In the second stage of transformation, Owen changes from shell-shocked patient into fierce and eloquent poet who can *express* and dramatize what most veterans experienced in silent terror: the texture, details, and incidents of trench warfare and, inside the self, the symptoms of what we now call post-traumatic stress disorder. Not only did his poems rescue him and his hellish experience from the numbed silence Benjamin describes; they also took back the experience of war from the jabbering propagandists and patriots, who glorified and falsified it for their own purposes. In such vivid, visceral poems as "Strange Meeting," "The Show," "S.I.W.," and "Disabled," Owen paved the way for soldier-poets after him. Showed them that they could, with luck and courage, incorporate their experience into poems and give voice to what they had gone through and the trauma they continued to endure long after the initial nightmare of combat.

CHAPTER FIFTEEN

The Quest and the Dangerous Path

As we approach our final trio of poets, we enter the contemporary world. These poets have read Freud and Jung and others. They know that the spiritual and emotional quests for meaning that began with such naive force in Romanticism have now been eroded by the skepticism and insights of psychoanalysis. The imagination of these three poets persists in mining what can seem at first like little more than a ribbon of neurotic themes crossing the rock face of an individual life. But as it digs down into the dark, unpromising rock, it still manages to extract what will become a bright shining.

IT COULD BE said of Sylvia Plath (1932–1963) that she was an enormously talented lyric poet whose determination to succeed was as powerful as her linguistic gifts. But talent and willpower combined would not have led her to self-transformation nor presented her with the challenge to recreate herself in and through language. For that matter, her transformation was not a broad and comprehensive one. Quite the contrary: it was narrow and highly focused. Or at least that aspect of it that seems to me to have made a significant contribution to human possibility in our culture. Her claim to a place in this brief list of transformative poets rests primarily on her poem "Lady Lazarus." I read "Lady Lazarus" as a poem in which a shattered self is reduced by male violence to nothing (to "ash") and then is miraculously (some would say diabolically) reconstituted as a mythic and powerful female figure: Lady Lazarus. This figure is a fusion of sexual power and magical resurrection. In her, we see both Lady Godiva—beautiful, self-dramatizing, and naked, parading before the multitude in such radiance that people cannot look or can only gaze with terrified awe—and Lazarus, the dead man returned from the grave by Christ's magic.

To a lesser degree, I am thinking of a parallel poem, "Daddy." The two poems address the dynamic relationship between men and women as one of violence and power. In both poems, the women, initially, are less powerful and are victims of male violence or collaborators in their own degradation ("Every woman loves a fascist"). Eventually, however, the transformation is from powerlessness to power and, in particular, to a special form of emotional power I would call "wrath." Wrath as a form of personal power is most eloquently praised by William Blake, who places it among his "infernal" virtues in the "Proverbs of Hell" section of his masterpiece, *The Marriage of Heaven and Hell*. There, Blake turns Christian virtues upside down and inside out, announcing:

> The pride of the peacock is the glory of God.
> The lust of the goat is the bounty of God.
> The wrath of the lion is the wisdom of God.
> The nakedness of woman is the work of God.

Elsewhere in the proverbs, he writes: "The tygers of wrath are wiser than the horses of instruction." When I declare wrath to be a significant human possibility, I am defining it as follows: wrath is the power of the powerless. For me, wrath necessarily has its origins in a recognition of one's powerlessness and the energy released by that recognition. Whether one can go on to utilize that energy of wrath to change the material conditions and relationships that render one powerless is another matter. My sense is that wrath can be a necessary stage toward further transformations and empowerment, that it can inspire us to take crucial risks.

Wrath is also anger focused into a single beam of energy, whose purpose, in poetry at least, is less to annihilate than to illuminate starkly what it focuses on. In "Lady Lazarus," this energy beam is focused on the victimization of women by men—a phenomenon so pervasive in our culture that it has been rendered invisible. Until Plath gave it this eloquent and unforgettable expression, it had mostly escaped dramatization by lyric poetry. A wrath that illuminates the topic. A wrath that empowers and transforms the victim self into a mythic figure: from little golden product of male alchemical power into an autonomous creature who returns from the dead and devours those who have harmed it.

It's amusing to see the discomfort with which many male critics continue to read Plath's poem, as if their task was to protect readers from its dangers and irrationality. Almost all my experience in decades of teaching has been in the opposite direction. I have seen innumerable young women who have felt the transformative energy of hope and courage from "Lady Lazarus." They've felt that the poem articulates what they have frequently experienced in relationships. It's my sense that Plath's poem can be a crucial stage in a young woman's awareness of power relations between the sexes. Having said that, I must add that I have seldom met a reader for whom Plath's poem becomes a permanent centering poem, a permanent touchstone of their being. It seems to function best as a stepping-stone: solid, true, grounded in earned experience, liberating, but not a place where one could stand indefinitely.

That "Lady Lazarus" emerges from Plath's traumatic life experience is only too established, since Plath is one of those poets whose lives are taken to be emblematic of larger issues. There is a danger, however, that the biographical legend can overwhelm the poetry itself. We know (she knew) that her father's death when she was eight was traumatic for her. We know that she, as a child, interpreted his death as his rejecting her and being angry at her. We know that the poems of *Ariel* (including "Daddy" and "Lady Lazarus") were in part attempts to integrate and dramatize the torment occasioned by the collapse of her marriage to the poet Ted Hughes. We know that in her imagination she fused her father's "betrayal" by dying with her husband's betrayal by infidelity to form a vision of women's agonizing suffering at the hands of men. This is her traumatic source, only too well documented. There's nothing to add to it, little of importance to say about it beyond the clear acknowledgment of its formative significance. My point is simple: the trauma of betrayal, which threatened to annihilate her, was transformed into enduring poems of energizing and affirmative wrath.

LIKE PLATH, STANLEY KUNITZ (born 1905) is quite conscious of struggling to transform traumatic life experience into affirmative self-creation, an ambition he refers to as "converting life into legend." In Kunitz's case the life experience was quite dismaying: his father committed suicide while Kunitz was still in the womb. His mother, furious at her husband's violent "desertion," would not allow the father's name to be spoken. When Kunitz was eight years old, his mother remarried, but this beloved stepfather also died when Kunitz was only fourteen. The absence of a father figure haunted Kunitz's life and, converted into the transpersonal significance of "legend," became a central theme of his work: "the son's quest for the father." In a boy, the quest for the (missing) father is a form of quest for one's self (think of Telemachus in the *Odyssey*). Father is sponsor, mentor, guide. His absence leaves a boy wanting in all those essential, existential categories.

In the poem "Father and Son," Kunitz directly addresses his father (here, a ghost), seeking, as sons will, answers, explanations, and guidance:

> At the water's edge, where the smothering ferns lifted
> Their arms, "Father!" I cried, "Return! You know
> The way. I'll wipe the mudstains from your clothes;
> No trace, I promise, will remain. Instruct
> Your son, whirling between two wars,
> In the Gemara of your gentleness,
> For I would be a child to those who mourn
> And brother to the foundlings of the field
> And friend of innocence and all bright eyes.
> O teach me how to work and keep me kind."

Given the purpose of the personal lyric as a means of helping individual selves cope with existential crises, such a powerful encounter as father-son (or mother-daughter, or other variations on these primary family relationships) would seem to be obviously rich in possibility and psychological necessity. And yet, to the best of my knowledge, Kunitz's poem (published in 1942) is the first lyric in English in which a son directly addresses his father. Certainly, once Kunitz's "Father and Son" was published, it was followed shortly thereafter by his friend Theodore Roethke's "My Papa's Waltz" and somewhat later by Dylan Thomas's "Do Not Go Gentle into That Good Night" (1952). Since then, the theme of direct or indirect child-parent encounter has become the focus of innumerable important poems in English as various poets have sought to dramatize the traumatic or emotionally powerful events of their childhood and adolescence.

Another traumatic dynamic in the Kunitz household was the mother's anger and unresponsiveness. According to Kunitz, his mother frequently told him he would be an outstanding success, but she never once kissed him and she never once, in his memory, smiled. This maternal grimness was another motive for the child's search for the father. In the following poem set in the family context, the search for the father has some success, but the son must pay a high price:

The Portrait

My mother never forgave my father
for killing himself,
especially at such an awkward time
and in a public park,
that spring
when I was waiting to be born.
She locked his name
in her deepest cabinet
and would not let him out,
though I could hear him thumping.
When I came down from the attic
with the pastel portrait in my hand
of a long-lipped stranger
with a brave moustache

and deep brown level eyes,
she ripped it into shreds
without a single word
and slapped me hard.
In my sixty-fourth year
I can feel my cheek
still burning.

The poem concerns a portrait, but it is also itself a portrait of a family triangle (mother, missing father, child) that concentrates powerful, perverse energy on the child as he struggles to understand who he is and how to make a necessary and nourishing connection with the father. The slapped cheek that is "still burning" in the speaker's sixty-fourth year is not simply an emblem of the persistence of shame at ancient humiliation, but also a covert symbol of the son's successful link to the lost father: they both have "hurts" (an implied suicide wound, a slapped cheek); they both have deeply offended an angry woman.

In a parallel poem told at a more "legendary" level, Kunitz is still a child figure whose spiritual task is to overcome adverse parental circumstances and become a vital and feeling adult. The poem's opening line, "My name is Solomon Levi," comes from an anti-Semitic song of Kunitz's childhood and thus alludes to yet another hostile force arrayed against the self's growth:

An Old Cracked Tune

My name is Solomon Levi,
the desert is my home,
my mother's breast was thorny,
and father I had none.

The sands whispered, *Be separate*,
the stones taught me, *Be hard*.
I dance, for the joy of surviving,
on the edge of the road.

In Kunitz's "legends" the plot, like that of many fairy tales, is the story of a young man (or woman) who must learn life lessons through adventures and misadventures.

Sometimes Kunitz's quest poems arrive at an existential grandeur, as in "King of the River." The title sounds very much like the title of a fairy tale, but it also refers to the northwest king salmon, the last stage of whose life cycle provides the dramatic structure for the poem. Here, the salmon struggling upriver to spawn is an emblem of the self driven by instinctual demands and yet craving spiritual and emotional rewards beyond the merely biological. It is an incantatory hymn of the anguished self trapped in its body and yet aspiring to transcendent principles, pleasures, and powers:

> If the water were clear enough,
> if the water were still,
> but the water is not clear,
> the water is not still,
> you would see yourself,
> slipped out of your skin,
> nosing upstream,
> slapping, thrashing,
> tumbling
> over the rocks
> till you paint them
> with your belly's blood:
> Finned Ego,
> yard of muscle that coils,
> uncoils.
>
> If the knowledge were given you,
> but it is not given,
> for the membrane is clouded
> with self-deceptions
> and the iridescent image swims
> through a mirror that flows,
> you would surprise yourself

in that other flesh
heavy with milt,
bruised, battering toward the dam
that lips the orgiastic pool.

Come. Bathe in these waters.
Increase and die.

If the power were granted you
to break out of your cells,
but the imagination fails
and the doors of the senses close
on the child within,
you would dare to be changed,
as you are changing now,
into the shape you dread
beyond the merely human.
A dry fire eats you.
Fat drips from your bones.
The flutes of your gills discolor.
You have become a ship for parasites.
The great clock of your life
is slowing down,
and the small clocks run wild.
For this you were born.
You have cried to the wind
and heard the wind's reply:
"I did not choose the way,
the way chose me."
You have tasted the fire on your tongue
till it is swollen black
with a prophetic joy:
"Burn with me!
The only music is time,
the only dance is love."

If the heart were pure enough,
but it is not pure,
you would admit

that nothing compels you
any more, nothing
at all abides,
but nostalgia and desire,
the two-way ladder
between heaven and hell.
On the threshold
of the last mystery,
at the brute absolute hour,
you have looked into the eyes
of your creature self,
which are glazed with madness,
and you say
he is not broken but endures,
limber and firm
in the state of his shining,
forever inheriting his salt kingdom,
from which he is banished
forever.

THE FRENCH ANTHROPOLOGIST Claude Lévi-Strauss once defined neurosis as a "monomyth." I take him to mean that it is a story shared by only a single person, the suffering neurotic, as opposed to ordinary myths, which are stories shared by a group of individuals and functioning as a bond between them. According to this thinking, a neurotic is isolated by the peculiarities of his or her story/background and cannot break out of this isolation into the larger, shared and shareable, human story.

In his best poems, Kunitz clings to the particulars of his experience and yet locates within them archetypal patterns that characterize a more deeply shared human questing. Thus in "The Magic Curtain," Kunitz tells the narrative of a boyhood in which he is companioned by his mother's young and mischievous maid, who, instead of delivering him to school, takes him to movie theaters where they share a passion for the actresses of the silent screen. Later the maid disappears, and, as we might expect, the mother never forgives her. But in this simple story, several legends are hidden. In one, a boy is trying to arrive at erotic awareness by evading the stern and ungenerous mother. In another, we have a legend of loss and recovery—the maid disappears and her disappearance is both explicable (she runs off with someone else's daddy) and mythic (she has disappeared into the Underground, the land of the dead). This subtle play between the mundane and the mythic liberates an enormous affirmative energy from what could be a sad story.

"The Magic Curtain" even manages to engage the world of history. Near its end, the maid sends a postcard from Dresden "after the war." Although this would, strictly speaking, refer to World War I, many of us know Dresden as a civilian city destroyed with horrendous loss of life during an Allied bombing at the close of World War II. The poem sets the single word written on the maid's postcard—"Liebe" (love)—against the massive devastations of war and the acute, intimate devastations of an unloving mother. At the heart of the poem is the question of how to forgive, how to love, how to keep the feeling self alive in spite of absence and deprivation of love. It is Kunitz's genius to discover such major spiritual projects in such apparently unpromising autobiographical material.

THEODORE ROETHKE (1908–1963), along with a number of his contemporaries—notably Robert Lowell and Delmore Schwartz—experienced the classical symptoms of manic-depressive or bipolar illness. Manic-depressive illness usually consists of initial manic phases of extreme alertness, mental and physical excitement and energy that can go on for some while, which then gradually or suddenly turn into depressive phases in which the patient feels overwhelmed by bottomless despair, lethargy, and suicidal impulses. Typical onset is in late adolescence or young adulthood, and the condition is interspersed with long periods during which the patient is fine. The disease is progressive, however, and the bouts of mania and depression often become more frequent and more severe as the patient grows older. Although it is possible to experience the manic phase as having some elements of pleasure and excitement, this phase can also lead to violence and destructive, impulsive behavior that can destroy a patient's work and personal relationships, financial stability, and health.

Roethke endured the condition in his life, and it wreaked its havoc there. As he rose into the manic phase, he was sometimes able to scribble disconnected lines and phrases that came to him on scraps of paper, but he had no more ability to control the illness than any other patient. And yet, though it caused him untellable agony, Roethke intuited that something could be gleaned from his suffering. Unlike many sufferers, he was prone to identify some aspects of the manic phase with a sense of ecstatic and mystical exaltation. And even the descent could elicit this respect: "In a dark time, the eye begins to see." He rose into mania; he plummeted into paralyzing depression. In his day, pharmaceutical treatment was unavailable (later came lithium and other medications). There was no medical solution, no therapeutic solution to his suffering.

In the world of reality, Roethke could only seek what treatment was available and dread the next onset of madness. But in the world of imagination, when he was stable, he took control of his illness by writing a series of lyrics that created imaginative parallels to the extreme emotional arcs of the manic-depressive cycle. This sequence, known as "The Lost Son," consists (according to his note to the *Collected Poems*) of eight extended lyrics, beginning with "The Lost Son" and progressing through "The Long Alley," "A Field of Light," "The Shape of the Fire," "Praise to the End!", "Unfold! Unfold!", "I Cry, Love! Love!", and concluding with "O, Thou Opening, O." Each of these poems can best be read as following the arc of a typical episode of illness, *except* for one crucial difference. Instead of structuring his poem in a way that mimicked the illness by beginning with mania/joy and proceeding to despair/depression, Roethke *reversed* the process. Writing with intimate knowledge of his terrible condition, he *rewrote* that condition toward a credible but difficult affirmation. He began each poem with an initial intense encounter with despair and moved toward a kind of peace and serenity that even had elements of joy and hope in it. As Roethke himself put it in an early description of the sequence, in "more difficult passages . . . the mind, under great stress, roves far back into the subconscious, later emerging into the 'light' of more serene and euphoric passages at the end of each phase of experience" *(On the Poet and His Craft).* Thus "The Lost Son," the first poem in the sequence, opens with these haunted lines "located" in a cemetery (although obviously they are more precisely located inside the mind of the speaker):

> At Woodlawn I heard the dead cry:
> I was lulled by the slamming of iron,
> A slow drip over stones,
> Toads brooding in wells.
> All the leaves stuck out their tongues;
> I shook the softening chalk of my bones,
> Saying,
> Snail, snail, glister me forward,
> Bird, soft-sigh me home,
> Worm be with me.
> This is my hard time.
>
> Fished in an old wound,
> The soft pond of repose;
> Nothing nibbled my line,
> Not even the minnows came.
>
> Sat in an empty house
> Watching shadows crawl,
> Scratching.
> There was one fly.

From such a solemn and grim beginning the poem finally arrives at these images of provisional hope and possibility:

> Light traveled over the wide field;
> Stayed.
> The weeds stopped swinging.

The mind moved, not alone,
Through the clear air, in the silence.

> Was it light?
> Was it light within?
> Was it light within light?
> Stillness becoming alive,
> Yet still?

A lively understandable spirit
Once entertained you.
It will come again.
Be still.
Wait.

Other poems in the sequence begin with equally morbid and cryptic images and move, by poem's end, to even more affirmative gestures:

My heart lifted up with the great grasses;
The weeds believed me, and the nesting birds.
There were clouds making a rout of shapes crossing a windbreak of
    cedars,
And a bee shaking drops from a rain-soaked honeysuckle.
The worms were delighted as wrens.
And I walked, I walked through the light air;
I moved with the morning.
("A Field of Light")

Roethke's genius (and courage) was to recast his agonizing medical illness into a poem with redemptive powers.

Roethke also was deeply responsive to the natural world. An heir of Wordsworth, he worked his own, ecstatic variation on the sustaining relationship the Romantic poet had pioneered. For Roethke, the beauty of nature held out personal comfort. He was propelled toward nature in part by an inescapable sense of self-loathing and vulnerability. Haunted by his own harsh feelings about himself,

Roethke used nature as a solace and imagination as a release. A large, unbeautiful man, he longed to be freed from his corporeal self and his inner anxieties and shames, to be united with the small and graceful shapes he found in nature—a vine, a small bird, a minnow, a snail—things that moved "as the spirit moves." This variation on sympathetic identification, by which he "became" those things that filled him with wonder, animates such poems as "Snake":

> I felt my slow blood warm.
> I longed to be that thing,
> The pure, sensuous form.

He had an intuition that, if he could slip out of his skin and become these tiny, other things (even things that might at first seem repulsive), he would become part of a deep, primordial process and healing would take place:

> I study the lives on a leaf: the little
> Sleepers, numb nudgers in cold dimensions,
> Beetles in caves, newts, stone-deaf fishes,
> Lice tethered to long limp subterranean weeds,
> Squirmers in bogs,
> And bacterial creepers
> Wriggling through wounds
> Like elvers in ponds,
> Their wan mouths kissing the warm sutures,
> Cleaning and caressing,
> Creeping and healing.
> ("The Minimal")

> All things are vulnerable, still;
> The soul has its own shine and shape;
> And the vine climbs;
> And the great leaves cancel their stems;
> And sinuosity
> Saves.
> ("Song")

This is courage speaking. This is the imagination announcing its hopes. It is a voice that calls us forward, out of our sorrow and suffering. Despite all his hard-earned personal knowledge of the devastation that such an illness can bring (or that life itself can bring), Roethke insists on his vision:

What else to say?
We end in joy.
("The Moment")

CHAPTER SIXTEEN

Constellations and Medicine Pouches

While from the bottom of a well
Fixed stars govern a life.
SYLVIA PLATH, "Words"

These are the final lines of a grim and lovely poem that Plath's estranged husband, Ted Hughes, chose to place as the final poem in her posthumously published collection *Ariel*. It is an image that, to my mind, partakes of a double fatalism. The first fatalism is contained in the astrological rigidity the image proposes: we are ruled by our stars and have no free will. The second image is more subtle and consists of shifting those stars out of the broad and open night sky and placing them at the bottom of a well. The sense of confinement and claustrophobia (not to say despair) that this location communicates adds to the poem's grimness. It's almost as if the image was saying: the implacable and impersonal forces that rule one's life are not in the sky but deep inside the self, as at the bottom of a dark well. Plath's image and its implications are almost at the opposite pole of the affirmative self-transformation I have been celebrating in the preceding pages.

Nor is Plath alone in her skepticism and despair. Near the end of his long poem *The Waste Land*, T. S. Eliot writes this memorable pronouncement: "These fragments have I shored against my ruins." Eliot next quotes three or four individual lines from extremely disparate literary sources, phrases that have a special importance and significance for him personally. It is an image of someone using a plank to prop up a hut or house about to tip over or collapse. The speaker in Eliot's poem is trying to sustain himself through lyric poetry—exactly the project that this whole book has been describing, exploring, and celebrating. But the fact is, such a project doesn't work for Eliot. The resources offered by the writing and reading of personal lyrics were not enough to sustain Eliot and speak to his deepest emotional and spiritual needs. He simply didn't have the temperament for the secular humanism that animates the personal lyric, and soon after *The Waste Land*, he moved steadily toward religious consolation and such sacred lyrics as his *Four Quartets*. There, and in political and cultural conservatism, he found the stabilizing order he craved, an order adequate to set against the disorderings that he experienced within and without. Eliot, like a number of his fellow High Modernists, retreated from the individual engagement with subjectivity that animated his early work like "The Love Song of J. Alfred Prufrock" and instead embraced one or another version of the Overculture.

Still, Eliot was authentically anguished in his youthful struggle (and even sporadically in his later work), and he points us in the right direction: we *do* use fragments to shore up against the disorders that beset us. We actively seek out those poems and parts of poems (images, lines) that speak to us deeply and personally. We seek them out and use them to sustain us—to express our innermost dramas and to regulate them.

But what if we were to repudiate the pessimism in Eliot's ruins image, where the self is collapsing like a dilapidated house? What if we were to shift back to Plath's image of stars as powerful constellations but add to that image what Plath withholds: the dynamic and affirmative power of individual will? What if we were to say that the lines and images we love are like stars and that we make them into constellations by our own positive acts of imagination? That we *create* our own personal constellations out of poems and parts of poems we write or read? Such a constellation is an emblem of our individual self blazing in the sky. Creating this constellation, we are creating a picture of our deepest self and its concerns.

And we are free to add stars to this constellation as a new crisis happens to us. Or to create an entirely new constellation for that matter. We have that freedom and power. We needn't be a desperate Eliot huddled in ruins, pushing lines of poems into the chinks and holes in the self's hut. We needn't be a passive and defeated Plath who cannot shake off her early trauma and the sense that she is powerless against its destructive power. This personal constellation of our favorite poems and lines of poems "governs" our life in the positive sense that it regulates and stabilizes our life. It even sponsors self-transformation by guiding us toward an idealized self we might aspire to.

With the image of a constellation of poems we are back to the optimism of Keats, who writes an early sonnet about his excitement on first reading Homer's poetry that contains this astronomical image:

> Then felt I like some watcher of the skies
> When a new planet swims into his ken.

Keats's sense of wonder and discovery is crucial to the power and purpose of the personal lyric.

AND WHY NOT, with lyric freedom, shift images in this final paragraph: from starry constellation to Native American medicine pouch? A medicine pouch is put together by each individual member of the tribe and typically contains totems and emblems of personal significance—a pebble from a place where something important happened, a small stone carved in the shape of one's totem animal, an arrowhead, perhaps some pollen, and so on. It's usually worn around the neck on a leather thong. This medicine pouch symbolizes and constitutes a person's own magic and the power associated with that magic. The poems that matter most to you are like the contents of that pouch. It is no accident that they rest against your body, near your heart.

Appendixes

Appendix A: Sacred and Secular Lyric

There are numberless sacred lyrics that propose that the sufferings and confusions of the individual self can or will be assimilated into divine orderings. These ordering images tend to be "above" the self and its earthly habitat—we look up to see them, as in the opening of this poem by Henry Vaughn, a seventeenth-century English poet of sacred lyrics:

The World

I saw Eternity the other night
Like a great ring of pure and endless light,
    All calm as it was bright;
And round beneath it, Time, in hours, days, years,
    Driven by the spheres,
Like a vast shadow moved, in which the world
    And all her train were hurled.

Because they embody perfection, circles and spheres are frequent images of divine order, as when Pascal defines God as "a sphere whose circumference is nowhere and whose center is everywhere." And we hear the dream of the circle's perfect ordering elsewhere also, in the poignant longing of the religious song (and sacred lyric) "Will the Circle Be Unbroken?" I say poignant, because the song's chorus is framed as a question, rather than as the confident statement of Vaughn's image of the ring of light:

Will the circle be unbroken
By and by, Lord, by and by?
Will the circle be unbroken,
In the sky, Lord, in the sky?

Here is another example of a tumultuous sacred lyric, written by a near contemporary of Vaughn's, George Herbert. In Herbert's poem, the disorders of desire and greed and anger threaten the speaker's commitments to the sacred order of his life as a Christian priest:

The Collar

I struck the board and cried, "No more;
I will abroad!
What? Shall I ever sigh and pine?
My lines and life are free, free as the road,
Loose as the wind, as large as store.
Shall I be still in suit?
Have I no harvest but a thorn
To let me blood, and not restore
What I have lost with cordial fruit?
Sure there was wine
Before my sighs did dry it; there was corn
Before my tears did drown it.
Is the year only lost to me?
Have I no bays to crown it,
No flowers, no garlands gay? all blasted?
All wasted?
Not so, my heart; but there is fruit,
And thou hast hands.
Recover all thy sigh-blown age
On double pleasures: leave thy cold dispute
Of what is fit and not. Forsake thy cage,
Thy rope of sands,
Which petty thoughts have made, and made to thee
Good cable, to enforce and draw,
And be thy law,
While thou didst wink and wouldst not see.
Away! take heed;
I will abroad.
Call in thy death's-head there; tie up thy fears.
He that forbears
To suit and serve his need,

Deserves his load.
But as I raved and grew more fierce and wild
At every word,
Methought I heard one calling, *Child!*
And I replied *My Lord!*

Certain information about the speaker of the poem is essential to our understanding of its disorderings and orderings. The speaker, like Herbert himself, is a priest, and the collar of the title is one worn by Christian priests. Such a collar restricts the speaker's behavior as surely as a dog's collar and leash restrict his. In addition, there is another meaning of "collar"—it is also a pun (a favored poetic device of the sixteenth and seventeenth centuries) on the word "choler" or rage. And it is rage that animates the speaker throughout the poem until the very last lines. Between the two meanings of the title (priest's collar and rage) the drama unfolds. The speaker at the beginning of the poem experiences his ascetic calling as an oppressive order, especially in a material and materialistic world, and his rage is a disordering that promises to free him from this oppressive order and allow him to enjoy some of the sensual pleasures and rewards of this world. But, this is a Christian poem—a drama of faith and doubt—and finally the "raving" and disordered speaker is rebuked by a voice: a supernatural voice, the voice of God. As soon as he hears that voice (which, by saying "Child!", identifies the speaker's rage as that of a childish tantrum), the poet surrenders again to the sacred orders and restraints of his faith and calling and a proper (Christian) understanding of his relationship to his Creator, modeled on that of parent and obedient child.

It would be foolish to try to say much on the subject of sacred lyrics— they are an infinitely rich cultural resource for proposing or praising orderings, whether they are sung as group hymns or as individual utterances. Still, the key distinction between the sacred and secular lyric is this: the sacred lyric imagines order as "up there" (in the sky, in heaven, above the earth) or "over there" (beyond the door of death). Order is a divine attribute or is a manifestation of a god's or goddess's supernatural power.

In the secular lyric, what you see (and feel, taste, or touch) is what you get. The limits of the poem are those of space, time, body. The secular lyric is emphatically *this-worldly*. Even the personal lyric's one major exception to limits, ecstasy, only proves the rule. Ecstatic release from the body, as in Keats's "Ode to a Nightingale" or numerous poems in praise of fermented beverages or passionate love, permits the self brief escape from its burdens, but the body is nevertheless a part of *this* world. Even Baudelaire, tormented devotee of ecstasy, knows we cannot heed his advice: "Don't be martyred slaves of Time, get drunk forever! Get drunk! Stay drunk! On wine, poetry, virtue, whatever."

The personal lyric locates the encounter between disorder and order here, where we are born, live, and die, setting aside the transcendent solutions of religion (or philosophy). The embodied self that is the dynamic center of the personal lyric is committed to this world, but such a commitment does not deny the importance or reality of the spiritual. It merely insists that spiritual and emotional sustenance are to be found in the material world, as when Whitman incarnates Christian mythology in several unlikely candidates:

> . . . the mechanic's wife with her babe at her nipple interceding for
> every person born,
> Three scythes at harvest whizzing in a row from three lusty angels with
> shirts bagg'd out at their waists,
> The snag-tooth'd hostler with red hair redeeming sins past and to
> come . . .
> ("Song of Myself," section 41)

Appendix B: The Social Lyric and the Personal Lyric

There's a distinction to be made between two kinds of secular lyrics. It's important, even crucial, but it isn't scientific so much as intuitive. Once we've set the terms, a reader will know it when he or she feels it, and some people will feel the distinction differently in relation to different poems. It has to do with where the poet locates his or her ordering power, but it's not as obvious as when a poet draws the ordering power from an established theology or philosophy. This third source of ordering principles external to the self is what I call the Overculture: the governing value system of the political, economic, and social order to which the poet belongs. As I mentioned earlier in the text (the opening of chapter 9), I've borrowed the term from Sara Hutchinson, who was talking about the complexities of negotiating between the two worlds of Native American culture and the dominant white culture (the Overculture). For my purposes, the two worlds the self must negotiate are the world of personal memories and emotions and the surrounding social/political/economic world (i.e., the Overculture).

If you were to say that these two worlds are not clearly distinct, that the boundaries between them are permeable, I would agree completely. If you were to say that there is no distinction worth making, I would disagree. We can *feel* there is a way our self is unique: its memories, associations, experiences; what it feels like to be us. What Gerard Manley Hopkins called "my selfbeing, my consciousness and feeling of myself, that taste of myself, of *I* and *me* above and in all things, which is more distinctive than the taste of ale or alum, more distinctive than the smell of walnutleaf or camphor, and is incommunicable by any means to another man" ("Comments on the Spiritual Exercises of St. Ignatius of Loyola"). There's no easier way to demonstrate this issue of incommunicability than to try to tell someone we know a vivid dream we have just had. How impossible to get all the details across in the telling, not to mention the memory associations we have with various objects and actions in the dream. Usually, the most we can hope to communicate is a bare-bones narrative gloss.

And then there is another self, a self that also makes use of the personal pronoun "I" but has solved its isolation by identifying with social groups so that its "I" is almost a "we." We could call this a corporate identity as opposed to a personal identity. All of us spend much of our lives inside our corporate identities—be they institutional affiliations; political allegiances; gender, racial, group, or national loyalties. Such corporate identities are part of our social being and have enormous stabilizing power.

But when we encounter the pronoun "I" in a poem, we might ask ourselves how much of the poet's subjective self is present in the poem, and how does this self make its presence known? Do all "I" pronouns stand for a distinct personality, or are some of them simply linguistic markers for the social or gender group whose attitudes and values are the primary source of the poem's thematic orderings? And when a poet views him- or herself as a poet writing from a certain social class or group and *for* others in that social class, might we not suspect that the values and orderings are not the result of an individual struggle with the poet's own subjectivity but are instead already supplied, already at hand? Such a poet's "I" does not stand for his or her unique personality but for a self whose attitudes and ideas are derived from the group.

Borrowing the term from the critic Kenneth Burke, we could call such an "I" a "corporate identity" and the lyric in which it appears a "corporate lyric" or a social lyric. In a social lyric, the poet's subjectivity is held at bay, and the crisis is resolved in terms of a ready-made set of attitudes and solutions (if, indeed, the poem registers a crisis at all).

I'd argue that most lyric poetry recorded as "literature" is of the social lyric type. Why? Because the literary tradition, any culture's literary tradition, is in the keeping of its Overculture. Those who control political and economic power in a given culture determine what will be accorded the status of important poetry, and they invariably choose poems that mirror and preserve their attitudes and values. One of the main *social* purposes of literature is to encode the governing group's value system in preservable or memorable language. Thus even in oral cultures, where there is no written alphabet and only memory can preserve poetry, the Overculture manages to inscribe its values into the long narratives we call epics.

The social lyric is concerned with regulating and integrating the self into social behavior. Even when a subjective issue like the passion called "wrath" emerges in a poem of the Overculture—as it does with the wrath of Achilles that sets *The Iliad* in motion—such a passion is to be reassimilated into the social group's goals. Achilles' wrath is socially functional in a male warrior system that lives by battle and pillage. In fact, it is celebrated as the battlefield "frenzy" that makes a hero almost invincible once the fighting starts. But this wrath must be channeled toward battle with enemies, not bickering and conflict within the tribe.

The personal lyric, on the other hand, has an entirely different attitude toward emotions and passions. They are the heart of subjectivity and the heart of the personal lyric. They are the emblem and agony of our innerness. We suffer our passions, we ride their roller coaster through our lives. But it is only the personal lyric that takes them as legitimate territory for expression *and* feels qualified to make meaning from them, make them into meanings.

While we're back with the ancient Greeks, let me give an example of the distinction between social lyric and personal lyric. Grief is a powerful emotion—probably the one that most directly threatens the ongoingness of the grieving self. Surviving the loss of a loved one can be extremely difficult. Eros has tangled our sense of self up with theirs, or has tied our two selves together. This moment of death and the departure of the dead is a great jeopardy in human culture. All societies have developed elaborate strategies to channel the sad and dangerous energy of this transition: rituals and magic prayers and ceremonies to send the dead one on her or his way and to draw together and reinforce the living community. There are even lyrics called elegies that are designed to express the feelings of the living for the dead. These elegies are complicated: they are expressions of the eros bond even as they are an important effort to sever that bond so that the griever is not taken to the land of the dead also. Social elegies keep a safer distance from the risk of connection with the dead. Just as the minister, rabbi, or religious official speaks for "the community" during a mourning ritual, so the social elegy speaks from a safer distance. Not so the personal elegy.

Discussion of this point can't convey what the comparison of poems shows more forcefully. Erinna was one of the very few Greek women poets to be regarded seriously in her time, the fourth century B.C. All we have of her work is six poems and fragments. Three of them concern her dear friend Baukis, who died as a young girl, soon after she was married. Two of these elegies are in the form the Greeks called "epigram." Epigram was originally a four-line poem to be carved on the gravestone or stele to tell people who was buried there and perhaps a little bit about them. Later in Greek culture, the epigram became a literary form—written down as a poem, but often still keeping the brief, four-line form and the pretense that the reader was standing in front of someone's tomb reading the carved words. These epigrams are often excellent examples of social lyric, because part of their task is to relate the deceased to his or her community. Often the words of the epigram were imagined to be the dead person speaking, as in this eight-line epigram of Erinna's:

> Stele and my sirens and mournful urn,
> which holds the meager ashes belonging to Hades,
> tell those passing by my tomb "farewell"
> (be they townsmen or from other places)
> and that this grave holds me, a bride. Say too,
> that my father called me Baukis and my family
> is from Tenos, so they may know, and that my friend
> Erinna on the tombstone engraved this epigram.
> (trans. Diane J. Raynor)

In its dignity and emotional reserve and its concern with locating the deceased in terms of place of origin, the above exemplifies the best of the social lyric. By contrast, here is another badly fragmented elegy for Baukis also written by Erinna. You have to read across great gaps of lost language, but the different emotional tone of it will be clearly apparent, and it is this intimate and individual tone that identifies it as a personal rather than a social lyric. The poem was known as the "Distaff" because it refers to weaving (a woman's task) and because spinning was part of the game of tortoise-tag the poem mentions:

> . . . girls
> . . . brides,
> . . . tortoise
> . . . moon,
> . . . tortoise,
> . . . .

. . . in leaves

. . . .

. . . .

. . . I combed

. . . into the (wide) wave

with mad feet (. . . leaped) from white horses.

"Aiai, I'm caught!" I cried out; (becoming) the tortoise

(I chased you round) the yard of the great court.

(Grieving) for you, poor Baukis, I lament these things,

these traces . . . lie warm in my heart

still; those . . . we played are coals now.

. . . and of dolls . . . in the bedrooms

brides . . . And near dawn

Mother . . . for the weavers;

she went to you . . . with salted . . .

For little ones . . . the Bogy brought fear—

. . . Mormo wandered about on four feet,

shape-shifting from one thing to (another).

But when into the bed . . . you forgot everything

that as a baby . . . you heard from your mother,

dear Baukis; Aphrodite . . . forgetfulness.

Because of this, weeping aloud for you, I leave (other things):

my feet are not permitted . . . away from the house,

with my eyes (I may) not see you dead nor lament

with my hair unbound and wild . . . Blushing shame

rakes my (cheeks) . . .

but always before . . .

nineteenth (year) . . .

Erinna, dear . . .

gazing on the distaff . . .

Know that . . .

the spinning . . .

These things shame . . . me . . .

with virginal . . .

But looking . . .

and . . . soft-spoken

grey-haired women, those flowers of old age for mortals.

Because of this, dear . . .
Baukis, I weep aloud for you . . .
the flame . . .
hearing the keening . . .
O Hymen[1] . . . often . . .
and often touching . . .
all for one, O Hymen . . .
Aiai, poor Baukis . . .
(trans. Diane J. Raynor)

Despite the fragmentary nature of this second poem of Erinna's, it is possible to feel how utterly different it is from the first epigram. The urgency of address, the outcries ("Aiai" first voiced as childish joy/dismay at being tagged "it" and later that same outcry expressing grief at Baukis's death), the intimate memories of shared experience—all these are expressions of the individual, subjective self given form and focus in the personal lyric.

Writing poetry or composing songs that expressed grief for the dead was a woman's job in ancient Greek culture. Women were given significant roles at births, marriages (somewhat), and especially deaths. Even in the mourning songs, a distinction was made between *social* grief and *personal* grief. In archaic Greece, there were two kinds of laments sung over the corpse, both composed by women. The *threnos* was a collective, formal lament, sung by a chorus of female relatives, although one could also hire a professional chorus to sing it, a fact that highlights its less personal character. The *goos* was a personal lament sung by an individual, usually the person closest to the dead. According to Emily Vermeule in *Aspects of Death in Early Greek Art and Poetry*, the *goos* tended to involve a direct address to the dead. It recalled concrete, intimate details about the deceased, and it emphasized the emotional plight of the bereaved. Again, according to Vermeule, the theme of the *goos* was "the memory of the lives the two shared and the bitterness of loss." We've seen how moving such a personal lament can be in Erinna's "Distaff" lines, but it is possible to regard the personal lyric from a disdainful distance as does this male scholar, Robert Garland, when he considers the *goos* in *The Greek Way of Death*: "A study of surviving dirges suggests that they primarily afforded the bereaved an opportunity to indulge in shameless self-pity by bemoaning the effects upon their own lives occasioned by the loss of the beloved" (30). Mr. Garland misses the point of this existential crisis entirely. The wisdom of the personal lyric lament is to open the self to the full disordering force of the loss by recalling the intimacy lost (the eros connections) and expressing the grief so fully while trusting the ordering power of the imagination to contain it. What is at stake is the survival of the mourning self.

When, in *The Iliad*, Achilles feels he has grieved too excessively over the death of his closest companion, Patroclus, he upbraids himself for "womanish grief." To feel too much is to be unmanly, unworthy of one's place in the Overculture. Subjectivity is gendered in most human societies. When we realize that women were, until the very recent past, silenced—their voices not heard or preserved by the vast majority of the world's various Overcultures—we can see one of the important reasons the personal lyric is regarded as subversive, suspicious in the eyes of the Overculture. The Overculture is the guardian of the social self. It has little or no regard for the self as a unique individual, nor does it have much sympathy with the individual's struggle with his or her disordering emotions and deeply subjective responses to experience. The Overculture is like the old cliché of the psychotherapist who sees his job as making the person "adjust to" social norms. Yes, the therapist is right to do so. And no, the therapist is also wrong. It is the personal lyric that is the guardian of subjectivity.

Let's consider another example of the distinction between the personal lyric and the social lyric. It may be a little difficult to follow all of the lines and logic in the next two poems, because they were written over 340 years ago and the English language has changed a lot since then, but they are both "spurned lover" poems written by Sir Thomas Wyatt, an aristocrat diplomat and soldier who, among other things, brought the conventions of Italian love poetry to England by translating the poet Petrarch. Both poems concern ladies who are former lovers and now reject the speaker:

My Lute Awake

My lute awake! Perform the last
Labor that thou and I shall waste,
And end that I have now begun;
For when this song is sung and past,
My lute be still, for I have done.

As to be heard where ear is none,
As lead to grave in marble stone,
My song may pierce her heart as soon;

Should we then sigh, or sing, or moan?
No, no, my lute, for I have done.

The rocks do not so cruelly
Repulse the waves continually
As she my suit and affection.
So that I am past remedy:
Whereby my lute and I have done.

Proud of the spoil that thou hast got
Of simple hearts through love's shot,
By whom, unkind, thou hast them won,
Think not he hath his bow forgot,
Although my lute and I have done.

Vengeance shall fall on thy disdain,
That makest but game on earnest pain;
Think not alone under the sun
Unquit to cause thy lovers plain,
Although my lute and I have done.

Perchance thee lies withered and old,
The winter nights that are so cold,
Plaining in vain unto the moon;
Thy wishes then dare not be told;
Care then who list, for I have done.

And then may chance thee to repent
The time that thou hast lost and spent
To cause thy lovers sigh and swoon;
Then shalt thou know beauty but lent,
And wish and want as I have done.

Now cease, my lute, this is the last
Labor that thou and I shall waste,
And ended is that we begun;
Now is this song both sung and past:
My lute be still, for I have done.

They Flee from Me

They flee from me that sometime did me seek
With naked foot stalking in my chamber.
I have seen them gentle tame and meek
That now are wild and do not remember
That sometime they put themselves in danger
To take bread at my hand; and now they range
Busily seeking with a continual change.

Thanked be fortune, it hath been otherwise
Twenty times better, but once in special,
In thin array, after a pleasant guise,
When her loose gown from her shoulders did fall
And she me caught in her arms long and small;
And therewithal sweetly did me kiss,
And softly said, *Dear heart, how like you this?*

It was no dream, I lay broad waking.
But all is turned through my gentleness
Into a strange fashion of forsaking;
And I have leave to go of her goodness
And she also to use newfangledness.
But since that I so kindly am served,
I would fain know what she hath deserved.

"My Lute Awake" could be basically paraphrased as: I'm going to sing this one last song addressed to you. It's useless, of course, because you're cold-hearted and cruel and proud of trashing me and other guys, too. But, I'll get my revenge someday when you're old and alone and cold in your bed on a winter night. Then you'll be sorry; then you'll regret all that time you wasted making your lovers miserable.

With "They Flee from Me," on the other hand, it's as if the personal lyric breaks through the conventional or social lyric and a real figure emerges, a speaker whose voice impresses the urgent stamp of personality. For its time, it's a rare and beautiful poem surrounded mostly by social lyrics. In a sense, "They Flee from Me" is also the complaint of a spurned lover. A paraphrase might go like this: now women avoid me (my former lovers) who once sought me out, risked a lot to be intimate with me. They were like deer who put themselves in danger to eat bread from my hand (how vulnerable that makes the women sound). In stanza two, he recalls the specific relationship that wounded and thrilled him: one particular woman who let her robe fall and held him in her arms and asked, "So how does this make you feel?" (When she says "Dear Heart," she puns on "hart," a male deer—a pun that enlivens many sixteenth-century English love poems, along with its companion pun: "deer/dear.") But this intimate recollection is an acknowledgment of the speaker's own, continuing vulnerability—now *he* is the deer. It's no longer a matter of women taking bread at his hand but of his being "caught" in her encircling arms, "trapped" by his love and sensual excitement even more than his earlier female lovers were. And though he clearly cherishes the experience in his memory, he doesn't much care for how vulnerable it makes him in relation to this woman. In the final stanza, the speaker, who has already admitted that he himself was a fickle lover, now accuses this special woman of the same crime. It's as if he can't bear the feeling of vulnerability and retreats into the socially conventional theme of blaming the woman. "But since that I so kindly am served, / I would fain know what she hath deserved," he concludes with some bitterness and irony. These lines seem "outside the poem" almost, in the sense that they appeal, as it were, to a jury of his male peers. It's as if these final lines are the speaker's way of regaining control by retreating to the conventions of his time's social lyrics (i.e., the prejudices and values of the Overculture).

In social lyric, the "I" is in charge because the "I" isn't a real person, only a pronoun allied with a set of conventional attitudes and values, those of the Overculture or of the speaker's "corporate identity." In personal lyric, the "I" is only partly in charge—the disorders of subjectivity or existential crisis are also powerfully present and to be reckoned with.

As I say, both poems are spoken by spurned male lovers and both end with a kind of anger and desire for revenge (though the vengeance fantasy occupies the whole last half of "My Lute Awake"—twenty lines—while it only appears in the final two of "They Flee from Me"). How is it that the whole feel of "They Flee from Me" is different? Where does that difference in tone come from? Somehow, reading "They Flee from Me" one has a sense that the poet is speaking about something that *really* happened to him and that the hurt and vulnerability he felt has entered him deeply. Is it something in the rhythm that sounds like a person feeling genuinely? Is it the way the women's vulnerability in the first stanza is reversed in the second stanza so that the "special" lover who disrobes for him seems, paradoxically, less vulnerable than he is, more in charge: she asks the questions, she is the active one in the kiss, she "catches him" in her arms—as if *he* and not she were the quarry in the hunt? Or is it the way sexual and emotional vulnerability are linked in both stanzas—and in both cases connected to as timid a creature as a deer? Does the sense of "reality" and uniqueness of personal experience come from the way the speaker remembers so vividly the "once in special" experience with his beloved, as if particularity of detail was a sign that something was real and really happened, as opposed to the generalized events described or referred to in "My Lute Awake"? However it happens, Wyatt's "They Flee from Me" has the feel of emerging from and expressing the subjectivity and uniqueness of real experience, whereas the speaker in "My Lute Awake" doesn't seem to be experiencing the grief inside himself. He's held it at bay by generalizing his plight and the solution to it. Conventional male Overculture attitudes toward love and women allow him to control his disorder without ever becoming personal. He deflects the disorder with wit and attitude, never letting it get inside him. Nor does he release any unique utterance or information (secret?) that might also highlight his subjectivity and heighten his vulnerability.

The social lyric uses the attitudes and conventions of the Overculture to control its disorderings, whereas in the dramas of the personal lyric we have a sense that the self is thrown back on his or her own resources and must wrestle with real passions in order to master the poem's disorderings. The fact that both "My Lute Awake" and "They Flee from Me" were written by the same poet show that this distinction must be a matter of feel and of poem-by-poem judgments.

NOTE

1. Hymen is the god of marriage. From another poem we learn Baukis died shortly after marriage, perhaps, as many Greek women did, from complications during childbirth.

Appendix C: Incarnating Eros

> I realize that it is impossible for me to raise myself to the altitude of the stars, and that I am forced, therefore, to bring down the stars to my own level and to incorporate them in my own physical universe.
> DYLAN THOMAS, January 1934

It is not only religion that imagines and images order as being something high above this tormented earth, which seems to be ruled by flux, accident, and ceaseless change. Philosophy and metaphysics frequently propose orderings based on abstract concepts and principles that are said to exist outside our changeable, material world. For example, in Sonnet 116, Shakespeare gazes heavenward and locates there an idealized, unchangeable symbol for love. It is a star. In fact, it may well be the polar star by which ships in Shakespeare's day took their bearings and navigated on the open sea. Such an image of an "ever-fixed" and stable object functions as an ordering principle in a world of storm and flux where the human heart can alter as quickly as the weather:

Let me not to the marriage of true minds
Admit impediments. Love is not love
Which alters when it alteration finds,
Or bends with the remover to remove:
Oh, no! it is an ever-fixed mark,
That looks on tempests and is never shaken;
It is the star to every wandering bark,
Whose worth's unknown, although his height be taken.
Love's not Time's fool, though rosy lips and cheeks
Within his bending sickle's compass come;
Love alters not with his brief hours and weeks,
But bears it out to the edge of doom.

> If this be error and upon me proved,
> I never writ, nor no man ever loved.

The star, his metaphor for perfect love, doesn't change, doesn't even move. Serenely above it all, this "love" exists outside not only the timebound world but also the human world of embodied selves. It is abstract, transcendent—a philosophical ideal (notice that it is a marriage of *minds* that the poem celebrates, not bodies). Perfected, detached, its purity somehow sustains us and represents an ideal everyone can steer by. Such a love doesn't perish with the "rosy lips and cheeks" of embodied being.

A belief in metaphysical ideals, like a belief in religious orderings, is based on faith, and when that faith wanes poets must seek elsewhere for their orderings. In the West, profound cultural reorderings and displacements in the eighteenth century led many poets to lose confidence in such abstract orderings, and one manifestation of this was the rise of Romanticism. The most characteristic expression of Romanticism was the personal lyric, which became more and more secular as the self struggled with a subjectivity no longer understandable in the light of religion or metaphysics. To bring the struggle for orderings down into the timebound, secular world was also to bring it down into the human body. The English Romantic poet John Keats was a profound admirer of Shakespeare and learned a great deal about sounds from his poems. In one of his sonnets, "Bright Star," he "borrows" Sonnet 116's image of the star and its ideal quality of being beyond change (and thus something one can count on, something that can order one's world). He borrows Shakespeare's star, but he alters it and alters his relationship to it by trying to bring its quality of stability *down* into the timebound and body-bound world of human relationships. Here is Keats's sonnet:

Bright Star

Bright star, would I were stedfast as thou art—
Not in lone splendor hung aloft the night,
And watching, with eternal lids apart,
Like nature's patient, sleepless Eremite,
The moving waters at their priestlike task
Of pure ablution round earth's human shores,
Or gazing on the new soft-fallen mask
Of snow upon the mountains and the moors—

No—yet still stedfast, still unchangeable,
Pillow'd upon my fair love's ripening breast,
To feel for ever its soft fall and swell,
Awake for ever in a sweet unrest,
Still, still to hear her tender-taken breath,
And so live ever—or else swoon to death.

Much as Keats appreciates the steadfast quality of the star, he notes its isolation: its "lone splendor" makes it like a hermit monk. His desire to bring the star's qualities of unchangeable endurance down into the world of sexual intimacy, where he lies "pillow'd upon [his] fair love's ripening breast," has as its price an entanglement with change and death. The "ripening" of breast is an image of fruit and contains within it the frightening implication of rotting and decay.[1] How can Keats have both his sensual intimacy and his "forever"? How can he have the disorder of human bodies in time and also have his "still"—his unchanging quality? Questions without an answer—because Keats expresses his situation as a passionate, irrational wish, a longing, not a metaphysical dilemma he is obligated to answer with a philosophical idea. What Keats's sonnet does is dramatize his longing for order *and* his longing for erotic intimacy, plus his sense that somehow they are at odds with each other. Whereas Shakespeare's sonnet makes a certain metaphysical or emotional claim based on an abstract ideal, Keats's sonnet hauls the issue right down into the timebound human world of bodies and passions and makes no intellectual claim but simply articulates an anguished desire. As such, it is a secular personal lyric. Keats has moved down from the detachment and idealization of Shakespeare's sonnet to the embodied self, but in doing so he's becomes enmeshed in mortality.

Here's a third poem that continues our theme of "borrowing" and modifying from earlier poems. Written about forty-five years after Keats's "Bright Star," this poem by Whitman seems to have overheard Keats's sonnet and lifted from it specific images and its sensual tone. This time, the borrowing is of the imagery of "washing" and "still," and also that favorite Keatsian word "soft":

Reconciliation

Word over all, beautiful as the sky,
Beautiful that war and all its deeds of carnage must in time be utterly
  lost,

That the hands of the sisters Death and Night incessantly softly wash
    again, and ever again, this soil'd world;
For my enemy is dead, a man divine as myself is dead,
I look where he lies white-faced and still in the coffin—I draw near,
Bend down and touch lightly with my lips the white face in the coffin.

Whitman has clearly also lifted from Keats the image of the ocean as a
priest whose rhythmic tides are like a ritual cleansing of "earth's human
shore." Keats's personification of something as vast and shapeless as the
ocean is matched by Whitman's allegorical figures of Death and Night as
"sisters" who are "incessantly softly wash[ing] again, and ever again, this
soil'd world." Both poems personify cosmic forces whose rhythms (one
thinks of the "tide of night" as a recurring pattern) indicate an order almost
more profound than the human imagination can comprehend, but one that
seems in both poets' eyes to be benevolently related to human anguish.

Keats was writing about the mystery of erotic love, Whitman is taking
on that other great mystery: death. If death and war are the disordering
powers Whitman seeks to engage and order in this poem, then "time" is
imagined not as his enemy but as his friend. Time will obliterate all traces
of war and its carnage.[2] And the sisters Death and Night, like the "priestlike
waters" in Keats's sonnet, will further cleanse a world soiled by suffering.

Whitman's poem, like Keats's sonnet, begins at a great distance from the
physical world—but its distance is the abstraction of conceptual language
("reconciliation" the "word" that is "over all"), which is compared to the
same distant sky that the stars in both earlier poems occupied. Whitman's
poem is like a zoom shot in films—it starts with a wide shot (wide as the
sky) and moves relentlessly down and in, closer and closer to details. Before
we know it, we are in the world of human bodies: of the dead body of "my
enemy" and of the speaker's own body drawing near to that dead body,
bending down and "reconciling" with it through the gesture of a kiss.

If detachment and abstraction are aspects of the Thanatos principle, and
if an "enemy" is another human from whom one is cut off by hatred
and alienation, then Whitman's poem is about the Eros of an affirmed
connection ("a man divine as myself") and a gesture (the kiss) overcoming
Thanatos. Whitman's poem *embodies* its meaning through selves (the "I"
and the body of the enemy) and through the action of intimate contact as
reconciliation. Distance can be a metaphor for estrangement and detachment. Both Keats and Whitman *collapse* the distances that their poems begin

with and in the process affirm intimacy and embodied meaning. Whitman's gesture of intimacy transforms the social and political estrangement of war just as Keats's sonnet sought to transform the personal space shared by two lovers. Whitman's erotic gesture is as radical as that recommended by Christ when he adjures, "Love thine enemy as thyself."

If Shakespeare's sonnet accepted the Western philosophic legacy of a mind-body split and located its ideals in the timeless mind, then Keats and Whitman both heal that split by bringing meaning down into an embodied self.

It's not only Western philosophy that seeks to separate the ideal and the sensuous. Christian thinking over the centuries has made common cause with its own version of the mind-body split, only this one involves soul and body. In much of Christian thinking, the soul is immaterial, pure, superior to the body—in fact, the soul is seen as an element of the divine trapped or housed within the mortal body. In his extraordinary poem "Crazy Jane Talks with the Bishop" (1933), the Irish poet William Butler Yeats dramatizes the collision of two contrary views: the "sacred" order of the body-hating Christian bishop and the "profane" or secular vision of embodied meaning presented by "Crazy Jane" and her erotic commitments:

> I met the Bishop on the road
> And much said he and I.
> "Those breasts are flat and fallen now,
> Those veins must soon be dry;
> Live in a heavenly mansion,
> Not in some foul sty."
>
> "Fair and foul are near of kin,
> And fair needs foul," I cried.
> "My friends are gone, but that's a truth
> Nor grave nor bed denied,
> Learned in bodily lowliness
> And in the heart's pride.
>
> "A woman can be proud and stiff
> When on love intent;
> but Love has pitched his mansion in
> The place of excrement;

For nothing can be sole or whole
That has not been rent."

The bishop tries to frighten Crazy Jane with mortality, with images of death and bodily decay. He urges the conventional Christian commitment to a divine order in "heaven" as a reward for those who spurn the sensuous, mortal world. Jane responds by affirming that "fair and foul" (good and bad) are not that far apart; that love is of this world, and, even more vividly, that "Love" (the ideal, Shakespeare's ever-fixed mark) is incarnated in bodies, where the sexual organs and the excretory organs (fair and foul?) are startlingly close together. Her final assertion seems quite mystically paradoxical: nothing can be whole that hasn't been torn (rent apart). This certainly seems to affirm a secular sexual mystery. But it can even be argued that she reinforces her profane but passionate point with a series of outrageous puns: "sole" means intact and separate, but it is also a pun on "soul." "Whole" again seems to reiterate "intact," but also puns on "hole"—as in vagina and anus. Last but not least, these holes that remain whole are "rent apart," but there's also a possible mocking echo of the bishop's insinuation that Jane is a prostitute who "rents" her body. Together all these puns might seem so odd as to be improbable, but note how powerfully and humorously they reinforce Yeats's governing image of profane but mystical carnality. Yeats—who argued in a letter that man cannot know the truth, he "can only embody it"—has, in this poem, embodied his personal truth with what was, for his time, surprising anatomical frankness.

NOTES

1. As the cynical Jacques remarks in the middle of the cheerful love story of Shakespeare's *As You Like It*: "And so from hour to hour we ripe and ripe, / And then from hour to hour we rot and rot, / And thereby hangs a tale" (2.7).

2. It's worth noting that Whitman is writing this poem at the close of the American Civil War, when the issue of reconciliation had great significance for the entire country. Whitman himself had spent several years of the war working as a volunteer in Washington hospitals dressing and changing the wounds suffered by soldiers.

Index

The Life of Poetry

POETS ON THEIR ART AND CRAFT

Carl Dennis
Poetry as Persuasion

Paul Mariani
God and the Imagination: On Poets, Poetry, and the Ineffable

Gregory Orr
Poetry as Survival

Michael Ryan
A Difficult Grace: On Poets, Poetry, and Writing

Sherod Santos
A Poetry of Two Minds

Ellen Bryant Voigt
The Flexible Lyric

Made in the USA
Las Vegas, NV
18 July 2023

74914677R00146